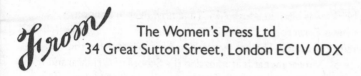

The Women's Press Ltd
34 Great Sutton Street, London EC1V 0DX

D0369594

Shula Marks was born in South Africa and now lives in London where she is Director of the Institute of Commonwealth Studies, University of London. She has lectured in African history at the Institute of Commonwealth Studies and the School of Oriental and African Studies. She has been an editor of the *Journal of African History* and has written numerous articles and books on Southern Africa, her most recent being, *The Ambiguities of Dependence in Southern Africa: Class, Nationalism and the State in Twentieth Century Natal* (1986). *Not Either An Experimental Doll* is her most personal book to date, the one in which she found herself most personally involved. She was able to meet Lily Moya's family and obtain their approval of the final draft of the book.

Shula Marks (editor)

Not Either An Experimental Doll

The Separate Worlds of three South African Women

The Women's Press

First published in Great Britain by The Women's Press Limited 1987
A member of the Namara Group
34 Great Sutton Street, London EC1V 0DX

First published in South Africa by Killie Campbell Africana Library,
Durban and The University of Natal Press, Pietermaritzburg, 1987

British Library Cataloguing in Publication Data

Lily
    Not either an experimental doll.
    1. South Africa—Social life and customs
    I. Title   II. Palmer, Mabel   III. Marks, Shula
    968.05'6   DT761
    ISBN 0-7043-4048-8

Printed and bound by Hazell, Watson & Viney Ltd, Aylesbury,
Bucks.

I turn to history not for lessons in hope, but to confront my experience with the experience of others and to win for myself something which I should call universal compassion – a sense of responsibility for the human conscience.

ZBIGNIEW HERBERT
Poland

Acknowledgements

The author and publishers are grateful to the following people and institutions who supplied photographs.

Mr and Mrs Eric Dahle, Durban: foundation stone ceremony, Lyman K. Seymour High School, Adams College; Mrs Bomback. Mr Gerald Dedekind, Agricultural Co-operative Action Trust, Pietermaritzburg: Transkei Homestead. Department of Historical Papers, University of the Witwatersrand Library, Johannesburg: Bishop Bransby Key; St Augustine's Church, Gibson's Boarding School; spinners at St Cuthbert's. Mr Alan Evens, Westville: Adams College prefects; foundation stone ceremony, Adams Teachers' Training College. Inanda Seminary: Sibusisiwe Makhanya with a class at Umbumbulu, from *Shine where you are*: a centenary history of Inanda Seminary, 1869–1969 (Lovedale, 1972). Mr & Mrs M. Martin, Cape Town: Adams Training College students. *The Natal Mercury*, Durban. Farewell service in Adams College Chapel. (The Editor is thanked for agreeing to waive the usual copyright fee.) All other photographs are from the Killie Campbell Africana Library and were found by Ms Colleen Butler.

The author and publishers also wish to thank Mr Bruno Martin, Cartographic Unit, Department of Geography, University of Natal, Pietermaritzburg, for the map of Transkei and Natal.

Contents

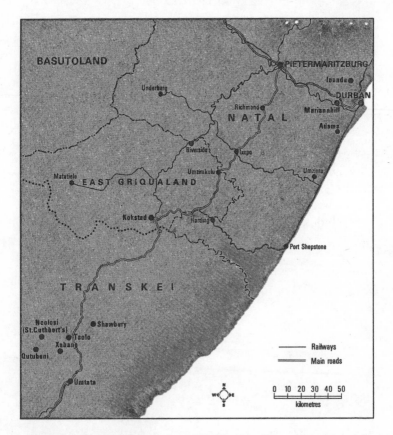

Map of the Transkei and Natal, *c*. 1950, showing places mentioned in the text.

Acknowledgements

Most projects in history, especially oral history, are collaborative ventures. This one, however, is indebted more than most to the enthusiastic and immensely generous help I have been given by numerous friends, students, colleagues, librarians and archivists. First and foremost, my debt of gratitude is to Lily Moya's mother and sister, who encouraged me to go ahead with the project and gave me and the oral historians who laboured on my behalf every assistance.* Attempting this project at long-distance, with only intermittent visits to South Africa was made possible through the kind offices of the Director of the African Studies Institute at the University of the Witwatersrand, Professor Charles van Onselen, and his talented and helpful oral historians, Manthe Nkotsoe and Dennis Mashabela, who recorded interviews with the family at an early stage. Moses ('Moss') Molepo, also of the African Studies Institute, and since tragically killed in Soweto in August 1985, at the beginning of a promising career as a social historian, not only accompanied me to Soweto but assisted on many occasions when liaison across the ocean proved difficult. This book is dedicated to his memory and to Lily Moya: both, in very different ways, victims of 'the system'.

At an early stage, Professor Tim Cousins, Dr Jeff Peires and Dumisani Ngewu all tried to find Lily on my behalf. Two South African journalists, Jenny Hobbs and Barry Streek, wrote articles in the local press in further efforts to trace her, and Dr Deborah Gaitskell gave me the invaluable advice which actually led me to the Moya family and wrote the necessary letters on my behalf. Halton Cheadle in the Law Department at the University of the Witwatersrand skilfully and generously negotiated the necessary

* Lily Moya is a pseudonym

legal aspects of the relationship with the Moya family. Rosalie Kingwill performed wonders in the Transkei in interviewing members of the family, providing me with additional information and colour photographs. In Natal, the assistance of Ruth Edgecombe enabled me to make contact with Florence MacDonald, and through her with a number of Mabel Palmer's colleagues and friends.

Researching the recorded material proved a little less taxing to my friends and colleagues, but here, too, I incurred many debts. Jenni Duggan and the staff of the Killie Campbell library, where I originally found the correspondence in the Mabel Palmer collection have been unfailingly helpful in providing xeroxed material and illustrations. Dr Sylvia Vietzen, who in the course of her biographical work on Mabel Palmer discovered the correspondence at much the same time as I did, and wrote a pioneering article on it, was most generous with advice and information. Mrs Anna Cunningham in charge of the Department of Historical Papers at the University of the Witwatersrand Library, miraculously produced unpublished and uncatalogued material from boxes in the basement at a crucial moment, and helped in finding photographs. The librarians at the Institute of Commonwealth Studies, London, followed up tiresome footnotes. Dr Christopher Saunders at the University of Cape Town and Ms Noreen Kagan Sher followed up clues provided by Dr William Beinart on the Native Labour Contingent in France and Lily's grandparents.

In 1982 I followed in Sibusisiwe Makhanya's footsteps in the United States, and consulted records in New York (the Phelps-Stokes Foundation records in the Schomberg Library; and records of Columbia Training College); Tuskegee, Alabama; Yale University, New Haven (Loram and Anselm Phelps-Stokes papers) and the Wiedner Library, Harvard (the American Board of Missions records). Here again library and archival staff were always friendly, interested and helpful.

I would also like to thank Mrs Ida Grant for showing me her own and Jack Grant's letters from Adams and Professor Alan Stone of Harvard University who enabled me to see records of the site visits to South African psychiatric institutions undertaken by the American Psychiatric Association in 1979.

There are many more debts of gratitude. I am grateful to

the Institute of Commonwealth Studies and the School of Oriental and African Studies for study leave in 1981–2, and to the School for the grant which enabled me to do much of the work on this project. Travel money from the Nuffield Foundation funded my visit to South Africa in July 1983, which was vital to the completion of the project. I have presented the material in these letters to seminars and lectures in the United States, Britain and Ireland – and have invariably learnt from my audience's response. I am particularly grateful to Dr Richard Werbner and Professor John Blacking for a variety of most stimulating suggestions, and to the late Dr Peter Sedgwick, whom I never met but who heard about the project second-hand and generously plied me with relevant and stimulating literature which I might otherwise have missed. This continued until the time of his own tragic death. Professor Terence Ranger and Dr Richard Rathbone kindly read the manuscript, made perceptive comments and saved me from some of my more erratic punctuation and exotic spelling. The comments of the reader of the manuscript for Women's Press were equally helpful and perceptive.

On various occasions, Lara and Rafi Marks scavenged in libraries and archives for me: I like to believe it will constitute useful training in research, but at least it was a source of pocket money. They, and other members of the family and friends, who have sat through – with varying degrees of tolerance – endless dinner-table conversations on the substance of the letters, the question of the right pseudonym for 'Lily' and the detective work involved in historical investigation all deserve a medal.

Joan Stevens assisted in typing the letters at an early stage of this project, and I am grateful also to Yvonne Crawford for her skilful assistance in its final stages. Last, but not least, Mobbs Moberly at the University of Natal Press has been tireless in her support for this project and a constant source of insight and encouragement.

SHULA MARKS
London, August 1985

Introduction

Some years ago, while working in the Killie Campbell Africana Library in Durban on the papers of Dr Mabel Palmer, one-time organiser of what became known as the Non-European Section of the University of Natal, I stumbled across a file of letters simply labelled 'Lily Moya'.[1] Somewhat idly, I flipped through, only to find myself riveted by the story which began to unfold. Quite quickly, I realised that the letters I was reading were a remarkable record of three exceptional women: Mabel Palmer, Lily Moya and Sibusisiwe (or Violet as she was known to whites) Makhanya. If, for most of the past in most parts of the world, most women have been 'hidden from history', black women in South Africa have been doubly hidden, both as women and because they are black.

But these letters not only recorded the at times discordant voices of three women, two of them black; in the case of Lily they were also the intimate and painful account of a young girl growing up in lonely and alien surroundings. They illuminate more of the South African condition than the majority of history textbooks; the generosities, yet limitations, of white liberalism; the nature of mission education; the socialization of black girls; and the dilemmas they confront. They also reveal the separate worlds which we all inhabit, but which are made more frightening and more separate by the divisions of age, ethnicity and race. The correspondence moves us beyond the aridity of an unpeopled political economy, to the ambiguities of everyday life. Yet through it we see the overarching constraints of social structure on human agency, and the complex relationship of individual psychology with a culture-bounded social order. If what is precious in the letters is the personal and the idiosyncratic, it is nonetheless possible through them to show that 'the private lives, even [the] obsessions of . . . individ-

1

uals, far from being simply psychological quirks or even aberrations, flowed directly from the social situation of these . . . individuals'.[2]

In a previous book, I have tried to use the lives of three individuals, Solomon kaDinuzulu, John L. Dube and George Champion to illuminate the workings of colonial domination.[3] The particularities hinged round an analysis of the state, nationalism and class. Significantly, perhaps, the voices were men's voices, the preoccupation largely with the male-dominated worlds of imperial pageantry and royal ideology, of state policy and petty bourgeois nationalism, of the migrant labour system, segregation and working class militancy. In some sense, this correspondence provides its counterpart: an entry into a more intimate and personal world where women's voices, articulating very different concerns with obligation and duty, philanthropy and welfare, sexuality and social control, are heard.

Through the letters and lives of Mabel Palmer, Lily Moya and Sibusisiwe (Violet) Makhanya, something of the differentiated meaning of the complex South African social order can be seen, a tapestry in which race, gender and class are densely interwoven. Unravelling these threads through the relationship of Mabel, Lily and Violet inevitably undermines any simpleminded feminist assumption of the power of 'sisterhood' in which the fractures of class, age and ethnicity are of no account.[4] Equally, however, it is a 'woman's world', shaped it is true by different forms of male domination, but in which men rather than women recede into the middle distance. And for all their differences, it is their passion for education which brings the English Fabian, the Zulu social worker and the Xhosa schoolgirl together across the chasms of class and age and race and destiny. As a result, this book addresses, in part, what is a burning issue in contemporary South Africa, the nature of black education and educational institutions.

I

The letters tell their own story, although it is important to know a little about the three women who wrote them to understand their full impact. When, at the beginning of 1949,

2

Dr Mabel Palmer received a letter from a fifteen-year-old African schoolgirl, Lily Patience Moya, from a postbox in Umtata in the Transkei, she was already in her seventies. Officially retired from her position in the University of Natal, she was still working, for a pittance, as organiser of the non-European section of the university. Born at Stockfield, Northumberland, in 1876, Mabel Atkinson (as she then was) was one of the first women to graduate from Glasgow University where she read philosophy and classics and studied in segregated classes — classes which were segregated by sex. She followed this up by completing a thesis on Scottish local government, inspired by the Webbs' work in England. This was for the University of Glasgow and the London School of Economics, where she held a joint research fellowship between 1900 and 1902. A scholarship from Mrs Bernard Shaw took her to Bryn Mawr College, Pennsylvania, after which she taught in a high school in Newcastle-on-Tyne and in Armstrong College (now King's College), Durham, before coming more permanently to London.[5] An early pioneer of working class adult education, she held a University of London and Workers' Educational Association tutorship, and lectured in economics at King's College for Women, in the University of London. She also worked as a freelance journalist, being the first woman after Harriet Martineau to write leaders for the London *Daily News*, then under the editorship of H. N. Brailsford.[6]

An ardent feminist, Mabel was one of a number of middle-class women intellectuals in the Fabian Society at this time, and played a major role in the establishment of the Fabian summer schools in 1907. She was a frequent speaker at suffragette meetings, and participated in 'every demonstration from the first "Mud March" to the great March of 1914'.[7] Yet, despite these political activities, her years in London were lonely, perhaps because her intelligence, outspokenness and strong will intimidated many of the men of her acquaintance. Margaret Cole describes Mabel Atkinson at this time as 'something of a stormy element in Edwardian Fabianism, a very truculent member of the Fabian Women's Group and a supporter of the Fabian Reform Committee'.[8]

Amongst the concerns of these years, as revealed by her articles, were such issues as the nature of the gold standard,

3

trade union affairs, and feminism and the problems of celibacy for university women. The last was a keenly experienced problem for Mabel herself, for she faced dismissal from her university job if she married, and would have been dismissed in disgrace had she been found to be 'living in sin'. She combined her intellectual and political pursuits with an internationalism which involved her in the early discussions amongst the Webbs, Shaw and Leonard Woolf on the constitution of the League of Nations.

Yet even in these early days, her philosophy was stern and strictly practical, well in tune with that of her Fabian friends. As she wrote on the final page of her treatise on *Local Government in Scotland:*

> We have passed out of the dazzling and blinding light of the dawn of which Wordsworth spoke . . . and have come forth into the plain daylight of our modern world. The earlier reformers had before them only the easy and invigorating work involved in the destruction of mediaeval doctrines and institutions. Ours is the far harder, the far less romantic task of slowly and painfully erecting fresh institutions within which this new society, based on the railway, the factory, the coal-mine, may live its life without self-destruction and self-demoralisation. Therefore our programme is less inspiring than the old. Our cries of 'Social Reform', 'Efficiency of Administration', appeal much less to the public than did the old shouts of 'Down with privilege!', 'One man, one vote'. The old Liberals needed mainly enthusiasm. Our work demands another temper — stern steadfastness, a somewhat cynical acceptance of facts as they are, a distrust of vague idealistic principles, and yet beneath that cynicism a belief that well-made laws and good administration will in time and gradually raise the nation from step to step. . .[9]

In 1914, Mabel married an Australian, who promptly joined the armed forces on the outbreak of World War I. After the war, she followed her husband to Sydney, Australia, but manifestly the relationship did not work out, and within six months she had left him and the Antipodes. In 1920, Mabel Palmer, as she now was, accepted an appointment as Lecturer in Economics at the Durban Technical College, which was later to become the Natal Technical College. In Durban, she took charge of the work of the WEA (Workers' Educational Association), which had been established in the College in 1915, for white workers. In 1931 with the opening of Howard College, she was transferred to the staff of Natal University College as Lecturer in Economic History. Mabel also rapidly became part of the liberal establishment, being an active member of the Joint Council movement, founded in the 1920s to promote discussion between black and white. In 1929 she joined the fledgling Institute of Race Relations. By this time, she was regarded as an authority on social and economic conditions among blacks in Natal, although it is clear that her knowledge of and sympathy for the Natal Indian community were always stronger and more sensitive than her understanding of the African majority, and that some members of the Institute found her as turbulent an element in their midst as had the Fabians in London.[10]

In 1936, Mabel retired from her lectureship and promptly launched into a second career, initiating the establishment of higher education for Natal's African and Indian population. Thus, she was directly responsible for much of the agitation and practical work involved in the setting up of a separate section of Natal University College for blacks. When its Council refused to allow classes for black students to be held on university premises, she organised (perhaps 'dragooned' would be more accurate)[11] her friends into running dual classes, initially in her own living room, later on in Sastri Indian College. These were held in the evenings and over weekends; in addition she organised annual winter schools for the students, modelled to some extent on the Fabian summer schools, at Adams College, the leading African high school and teacher-training and theological college, which had originally been founded by American Congregationalist missionaries at Amanzimtoti.[12] She reconciled these segregated classes with her conscience by drawing an analogy with the separated male/female classes which she had experienced in Glasgow in her youth. The majority of the students were schoolteachers, anxious to upgrade their qualifications and grateful for any assistance; for the time, they were prepared to accept the inequalities and humiliations of a separate and

5

inevitably unequal system.

Sylvia Vietzen, her biographer, pictures Mabel launching black university education in Natal:

> classes at inconvenient places and times such as Friday evenings, all day Saturday and Sunday mornings at hutments at Sastri College, reached in all weather by rickshaw; using her home as the office; giving her services free for the first three months, and for little more after that; submitting the balance sheets in her own hand on a yellow writing pad; lending her own books and forwarding the fees; subsidising the families so that individual members might study; urging not only degree candidates but ' . . . also . . . any person who merely wishes to extend his knowledge . . . ' to attend; urging, too, any student who might find it 'impossible to get to Durban to attend the classes' to be in touch with her for possible 'help in the way of books, tuition or advice'. Africans and Indians, many of them from remote country areas, came in trains and taxis and slept in doorways . . . to attend these classes.[13]

After World War II, the separate Non-European Section of the University of Natal was recognised institutionally, and Mabel became its official Organiser. At the same time she played a key role in the founding of the Durban Medical School for black students in 1949. By now, she was widely recognised by Africans, both inside and outside of Natal, as 'a friend of the natives' — a phrase I use with deliberate ambiguity. Edgar Brookes, ex-headmaster of Adams and liberal Senator representing African interests, who knew Mabel Palmer well, sums up her activities on behalf of the non-European section of the University:

> At all times, and especially at the beginning, the running of classes was up-hill work, [yet] Mabel Palmer, with a generous heart, and with a background admirably suited to an experiment in workers' education (which this essentially was), gave herself without stint to what proved to be the most significant task of a busy and useful life. Not unduly swayed by sentimentality, she saw the weaknesses

6

of her charges and applied a devastating common-sense to their complaints. Whoever knew of those days from the inside or has read up the voluminous correspondence about the non-European classes ... must marvel at her pertinacity, idealism and practical sense.[14]

As we shall see, a 'devastating common sense' and a lack of sensitivity, coupled with quite extraordinary generosity in both time and money, characterised Mabel Palmer's relationship with Lily Moya, whom she liked to describe as 'my little protegée'. The forthrightness was not a function of her old age in 1949. A revealing exchange of letters early in 1930 with A.W.G. Champion, the organiser of the large all-in black Industrial and Commercial Workers' Union, the ICU, in Natal and one of the most outstanding African politicians and entrepreneurs of his generation, is typical of her style. After asking Champion for early documents on the ICU, which she believed would be of value for the 'future historian of trade unionism among the Bantu races', for the time a highly perceptive and unusual request, she continued:

> I am sorry it has not been possible for me to see anything of you lately. The difficulty is that I cannot pretend that I think your present policy is the right one or ought to be supported.[15]

After suggesting that he clear himself of the current suspicions of 'financial slackness with trust funds', which had led to his membership being blackballed by the Joint Council in Durban, she ended 'I am very sorry for all the difficulties into which your inexperience has led you'.[16]

Champion, never one to take an insult lying down, responded in kind:

> In reply to your letter of the 13th inst. I wish to state that I am not interested in it at all. Why do you want to heap an insult on my injury. I do not care to be a member of the Joint Council of Durban. I am what I am ... and please do not always tell me what you think of me ....

> You should always respect my feelings, Mrs. Palmer, whether you are a European and I, a Native . . .[17]

It is perhaps revealing that although Champion left more private papers than any other South African black political leader, and they are scattered in several university libraries, none of them are in Natal!

Yet for all her lack of tact, the generosity of Mabel was also undoubted, as was her dedication to the cause of black and especially black women's education. Her ability to conjure up books and tuition fees was widely known, beyond the confines of Natal. It was this reputation, which she learnt of through a penfriend studying at the University of Cape Town,[18] that led Lily to write to Mabel at the beginning of 1949:

> I can be very pleased if you can take me in your college as a boarding student. I do not moralise when I tell you that I'm a helpless orphan. I have obtained this educational status through my being a daystudent, only due to my financial embarrassment.[19]

And it was probably the help and encouragement Mabel had had in her early years from people like the Shaws and Webbs, among others, and a certain amount of self-identification, that led her to respond to Lily's letters. As she wrote in April 1949 to the Native Commissioner in Umtata, the official responsible for the administration of the Transkei:

> ... the letters are very well expressed giving me the impression of a young thing straining at the leash with desire for some training to fit her to take part in the life outside a native location. When I remember the many people who helped me in years gone by to get the education which has enabled me to lead what has on the whole been a happy and successful life, I feel that I cannot shut my ears to her appeal.[20]

8

II

There were more objective reasons for Mabel to be moved by Lily's pleas, however. The central figure in these letters, she was in her own way an exceptional young woman; at the same time, she was a not atypical daughter of the mission-educated community which dominated African nationalist politics in twentieth-century South Africa. Although their forebears had been the prosperous Christian peasants and successful petty bourgeoisie of the late nineteenth and early twentieth century, this group came increasingly under fire after the Afrikaner Nationalists won power in the 1948 election. Indeed, during the very years that these letters were written a government-appointed Commission into African education (the Eiselen Commision) was framing the report on which the Bantu Education Act of 1953 was based. The Act was part of a broad strategy to defuse growing African nationalism and working class militancy through a school system which emphasized ethnicity and was designed to 'fit' Africans for 'their station in life'; it brought the mission schools which play so large a role in this story directly under government control for the first time.[21]

At the beginning of 1949 Lily was writing from the home of her guardian, a paternal uncle in Umtata, and about to take her final school-leaving or matriculation examinations. She was only fifteen — a fact which shocked Mabel when she discovered it and led to the long delay between Lily's first letter and her eventual admission to a high school in Natal. Although Lily did not pass the matriculation examination, it is salutary to remember that in the whole of South Africa in 1949 only 201 African girls actually went beyond the Junior Certificate examination (Std. VIII), and only 0,2 per cent of the African schoolgoing population actually passed the matriculation examination, which acted as the university entrance qualifi- cation. Most of these would have been male and far older.[22] In her final class at St John's, Lily was in fact the only girl, and six years younger than the next youngest student.

In 1950, the average school life of African children who managed to go to school — about a third of the possible number — was only four years; in the whole of South Africa, under 3 per cent of African children went beyond primary school. The vast majority of elementary schools were ill-equipped, without books or the necessary furniture. Teachers were 'seriously overloaded, extremely ill-paid and about 18 per cent of them were unqualified'.[23] The poor provision of schooling for Africans was not accidental. The dominant white attitude to black education at the time was well summarised in parliament by J.N. le Roux in 1945:

> [we] should not give the natives an academic education as some people are prone to do. If we do this we shall later be burdened with a number of academically trained Europeans and non-Europeans, and who is going to do the manual labour in this country? ... I am in thorough agreement with the view that we should so conduct our schools that the native who attends those schools will know that to a great extent he must be the labourer in the country.[24]

In the course of 1949—50, while she waited for Mabel to get her into a high school in Natal, Lily herself acted as a teacher in two Anglican village schools; with her educational background, she was better prepared than most elementary school teachers, despite her lack of any teaching qualification. The accounts of her experiences are amongst the most vivid in the correspondence.

Thus in August 1949, she wrote of her experiences at Ncambele village school where she acted as substitute teacher:

> It was a great shock to me, that I should teach. The Principal teacher was quite amazed — he did not know that I was so small, indeed, the students are very big in that school. ... Just imagine how I nearly lost my senses, how I shivered from toe to hair when I found myself standing in front of such big students, very old indeed for such classes. ... What would you have done if you would have been myself. Would you have gone to the classrooms or ran back home? This incidence brought a great change to this prolonged monotonous life. ...[25]

Some months later, in February 1950, she was called to teach at Qutubeni, again part of St Cuthbert's Mission, from Lily's point of view a real 'school in the bush':[26]

> Do you know what kind of a school this is? I mean to say it is a very hard job for me:—The school is newly established at a place where there was never a light of any sort of civilization. There is no church. The nearest one is a distance of five or more miles away. All people except the woman I stay with are proper heathens. . . . The place itself is surrounded by gigantic mountains. The country is stoney. It is as primitive as I think the old stories relate to us how the people were before Nongqause.[27] I never dreamt that there was still such a backward place. . . . P.S. I am just in the black hole of Calcutta and I don't like it at all.[28]

The influence of the Bible and local preacher on Lily's prose style are easy to detect. Mabel was sufficiently impressed with the 'lively and amusing way' in which Lily had expressed herself on the first occasion, however, to muse on the possibilities of her becoming a journalist and to ask her to write a short paper on 'The Life of a Native Girl in a Native Reserve' which she 'might try to have printed somewhere'. Two weeks later Lily responded. The result was hardly what Mabel expected:

> I'm very sorry for not producing a good draft to the 'Life of an African Girl'. I have not been a good traveller or very observant to such a subject, you will see little of my experience only based to what our people say to our girls and what we ought to do, to be preserved, divinely devoted and single-minded, expecting ourselves to be the future mothers, the examples to be admired and to be selfrespective of ourselves.
>
> We are frequently mislead [sic] by minor misdeeds. We never use our intelligence. We are flying for only outside admiration, our actions are rot, revealing our internal impurity.
>
> We have a thrilling audacity to do evil. We forget the meaning of the word 'girl', that a girl should be preserved.

11

We make people believe that civilization came with evil. Yes, we are people surrounded by stumbling blocks, things which look inviting. . . . We live only for the present but not for the future. . . . We are only advised to marry and as we grow we think of nothing else but marry . . .[29]

Mabel's response was frank and to the point, as ever:

I am returning herewith the paper that you did for me on the 'Life of a Girl in a Native Reserve'. It is not really very good. It is much too general and gives too little detail, and I think it is a pity that you devote so much time to describing the manners of some Zulu girls. There are a certain number of bad mannered girls everywhere.[30]

She followed this up with a series of questions to Lily on daily life in the Transkei. 'In what ways are little girls of seven treated differently to little boys say of seven years?', she asked earnestly, echoing the concerns of many a later feminist scholar. 'What sort of amusements do young adolescent girls have in Zulu Reserves? Do you often go to the Movies for instance? Do you go to dances?' she continued, inadvertently revealing her astounding ignorance. It is extraordinary, for example, that a woman so widely regarded as an 'expert' on 'natives' should have thought that the Transkei, the home of the Xhosa-speaking people, was a 'Zulu Reserve'; as striking was her total incapacity to conceive of the world which Lily inhabited. 'Imagine', Mabel continued,

that you are writing to an English girl in Durban about the same age as yourself who wants to know in what way your upbringing is different to hers. . . .[31]

At stake, however, was not only Lily's but Mabel's inability to 'imagine': Mabel's inability to 'imagine' not simply what it was like to be a 'young Native Girl growing up in a Native Reserve', but an impressionable adolescent growing up without a mother in an austere and sexually repressed environment, alienated from herself, her community and her kin. To understand this triple alienation, it is necessary to turn to the Anglican milieu of St Cuthbert's Mission, in which Lily was born and grew up.

III

The Eastern Cape has a tradition of Christianity going back to the early years of the nineteenth century. In the Mpondomise area, however, around Tsolo district where Lily was born, Anglicanism owed its origins to the activities of the missionaries Bransby Key and A.G.S. Gibson, both of whom were later to become bishops. Although Key first settled on the Inxu River and built his first wattle and daub church dedicated to St Augustine in the Tsolo district in 1865, he had little success until the territory was taken over by the Cape Colony in 1872. Even then, his main successes were amongst the Mfengu settlers in the region, and in 1880 the mission was burnt down in a Mpondomise uprising against the government which began with an attack on the Mfengu converts.[32] For Key the suppression of the uprising marked a turning point. As in other parts of the Eastern Cape, it was 'only as people became impressed by the final failure of their resistance, only as they found their feet anew on terrain which was no longer theirs, and only as the settler authorities demonstrated their power to dictate the terms on which future negotiation might be conducted, that education began to be sought instead of shunned'.[33]

A new site on the banks of the Ncolosi river was selected, and while his house and church were being rebuilt, Key lived and worked in a little village nearby: the home of Lily's maternal grandmother, Alice.[34] Alice's family were Mfengu converts to Christianity and her father is listed as a schoolteacher as early as 1884. The family of Lily's maternal grandfather, Daniel Mvamba, had equally close connections with the mission, and one of his sisters worked in the home of Bishop Key. So intimate was the identification that more than a dozen years later Daniel and Alice named at least two of their children after members of Bransby Key's family.

Daniel Mvamba was one of the first Mpondomise lads to enter Gibson's Boarding School at St Cuthbert's and by 1890 was the Superintendent of Boarders there, among the early Mpondomise adherents of the revived mission. A sister was among the first of the Mpondomise girls to enter Miss Blyth's Industrial School for Girls, which was attached to the Boarding School in the early 1890s, which Alice also attended.[35] In

1898, Daniel appears as headteacher and lay reader in the annual reports of St Cuthbert's Mission, a position which he held for many years. By 1902 he had been joined in his work by Alice.[36] Described by Father Godfrey Callaway, who succeeded Gibson as missionary and bishop, as 'a devoted and excellent preacher . . . a dear fellow and very lovable',[37] Mvamba was an energetic and successful teacher who identified totally with the life of the Church of the district.[38] Like their Mfengu relatives and neighbours, Daniel and Alice placed a high premium on education, the one mode of 'entry to the colonial order above the most menial forms of labour'.[39] Of their eight children, the four girls ended up as schoolteachers, while Callaway was god-father to one of the sons, who in turn became an agricultural demonstrator.

Daniel was not simply a man of the church however. He was also a local headman and cultivated substantial plots of land, on which he grew maize, melons, beans and pumpkins, a fruit orchard ('apples, peaches, quince and several kinds of plum') and grazed cattle. He sold his produce on the Tsolo market. By Daniel's day, peasant prosperity was heavily dependent on access to non-farming sources of income, which he would have obtained from his position as headman and teacher. At the same time his headmanship opened opportunities of power and patronage in the district; as intermediary between church and state on the one hand and the local populace on the other, Daniel was a man of considerable influence.[40]

Lily's paternal grandparents were also Christians and equal-ly prosperous and influential. Henry Moya attended the Mpondomise Boarding School and the college at Umtata at the same time as his friend Daniel, and like him taught in the diocese. He, too, later became a headman, and was amongst those from the region who went with the South African Native Labour Contingent to France in World War I. A letter in 1916 from France by one of his compatriots from the Eastern Cape, H. M. Tyali, to the Chairman and Members of the Transkeian General Council, is so delicately nuanced a statement of the ambiguities of this generation's situation, and so reminiscent of Lily's later prose style, that it deserves lengthy quotation:

14

... the whole Empire had had some doubts that a race like the Natives of South Africa who were disarmed and kept like little children would gladly accept the call from the King. Men of no weapon men of no training to any sort of fighting to go through the big waves and dangers of German submarines only trusting to God's help while our masters had trusted to God as well as to the manly strength. What do our masters now think? When a Native has shown his loyalty and good behaviour during the big war. ... Let the government to-day to think of a Native, let the Empre [sic] know that a Native of South Africa should be given a situation of better rights gentlemen. ... I therefore say myself today Government should be asked to push a Native to a higher stage. I should say a Native should not only be used and in use of working with the spade picks and axes so forth, he should be trained to something better for a knowledge. ... The necessity of a Native to be enlisted in the same rights with the white men to-day is seen. A Native should not only be looked as boy as it is now. ... I hope the House in dealing with this letter will not forget that a Native is loyal. Consider this gentlemen that it is the white race who rebelled during this War but all eyes were looking on Natives to rebel against the Government.[41]

In the first decades of this century, Henry Moya was, if anything, even wealthier than Daniel, producing gooseberries, strawberries and figs for the Tsolo market — or at least so the family recollects. He also had a few cattle and goats and some sheep, selling their wool in Tsolo.

Whatever the prosperity of her grandparents, Lily's own parents, Walter and Harriet, were decidedly less well-to-do. By the time they married, the possibilities of earning a living on the land had greatly diminished for Christian and non-Christian alike. Even in its heyday, prosperity through agricultural production had been restricted to a handful of peasants. Long before the 1913 Lands Act which restricted African ownership to less than 8 per cent of the land of South Africa, land shortage, the absence of credit, and state support for white but not black production, was foreclosing on this option even for this successful minority in parts of the Eastern Cape. The process was an uneven one: strains felt in the Ciskei in the nineteenth century were in evidence further east somewhat later. Nevertheless, by the 1920s, 'the mass annual exodus of male migrant labourers was a dominant feature of the political economy of the Transkei'.[42] By then, Griqualand East Christians were particularly hard-pressed and in the early 1920s, Tsolo district and neighbouring Qumbu saw scenes of angry protest against rising maize prices and declining yields, led by some of the 'wealthier and best dressed of the more enlightened and wealthy natives of the district'. 'Many of the Christian families were deeply in debt and they were threatened by an inability to educate their children — and hence by some difficulty in differentiating themselves from the traditionalist peasantry.'[43]

By the 1930s, the impoverishment of the Transkei was intensified by the impact of the world depression and 'both in traditionalist and "school" communities, it was becoming more and more difficult to meet subsistence needs through peasant production'.[44] For Christians the situation was aggravated through their adoption of new patterns of consumption, the premium they set on education and their acceptance of the cash economy and primogeniture in relation to property: it would seem that both Walter and Harriet found themselves excluded from family land by older brothers who were the sole inheritors of the family wealth.[45]

Thus, in the early 1930s, Lily's father was forced to seek work on the mines for the first time. Unlike an earlier generation of migrants who had been able to return home after one or two spells on the Rand, he remained there until the late thirties, when he left for Cape Town. He died shortly afterwards of pneumonia. Harriet struggled on in the Transkei, trying to support three children, of whom Lily was the oldest. The familial drive for education, together with Lily's own natural ability and application, ensured her scholarships at a bewildering succession of Anglican mission schools: St Cuthbert's, Shawbury, St Matthew's and St John's. The frequent moves were dictated by the educational possibilities available in each school. Perhaps not surprisingly Lily was later to describe her life as 'a transfer' from one institution to another, with little time for friends or play.

Unable to make a sufficient living by following her vocation

16

as a teacher in the Transkei, in 1948 Harriet left for Johannesburg in a desperate effort to find work — leaving the teenaged Lily with relations in Umtata just as she was entering her final school years at St John's, a boarding school for boys and a day school for the handful of girls who reached matriculation. In exchange for board and lodging, she was expected to take care of the household chores and the small children both before and after her day at school. Although this form of housework in exchange for board and lodging amongst kin is a not infrequent form of fostering amongst African families, in her letters to Mabel, Lily complained bitterly of the difficulties of her position. As her sister put it later, 'she was just taken as a servant', and not surprisingly her studies suffered accordingly.[46]

The only girl in her class, she was isolated and unhappy, and Mabel's letters became a source of hope and inspiration, their failure to appear the occasion of much lamentation, and disappointment lest her case be forgotten, her only line to the outside world severed. Thus after a couple of months' of silence on Mabel's part, in the middle of 1949, Lily was to write:

> It disappoints me too severely when you don't reply to me. I really don't know what to do now. I thought your answer to my letter would come earlier so that this time I would be busy with studies, I mean with reading the books.[47]

and, three weeks later,

> I'm really stranded. You seem to have completely withdrawn from giving me any help. I am puzzled. I cannot tell whether you are still considering my state of affairs as your promise in your last letter or have been completely desuaded [sic] by your advisers, against helping me.[48]

One can only sympathise with Mabel's somewhat harassed reply:

> You really must not become so impatient if you do not hear from me immediately. I am a very busy woman with a great deal to do for my own students, and it is only because your first letter appealed to me that I was willing to interest myself in your case . . .[49]

17

And Mabel did interest herself in Lily's case. With accustomed energy she set about enquiring of her friends and acquaintances what the most suitable arrangements for Lily would be in Natal, and sought to find funds for her from the Natal branch of the Association of University Women of South Africa, and from her more affluent friends. When these failed to come up with the money, she determined to pay for Lily herself out of her meagre salary as Organiser of the Non-European Section of the University — despite the fact that she would have to forgo a winter coat in order to do so. At the same time, she sent Lily the books set for the matriculation examinations: Lytton Strachey's *Queen Victoria*, *King Lear*, *Jane Eyre*. Neither Mabel nor Lily appear to have been struck by any incongruity in the cultural exchange. Drawn from a family which clearly shared in the Cape liberal vision of a common society, Lily identified fully with the western culture she was being offered. Despite the gulf between the vision and the practice even in the Cape, it was only a later, black consciousness, generation which questioned the validity of the vision.[50]

If there was much that was shared in this common western cultural inheritance which the Christian educated elite of South Africa had by this time made their own, there were hidden assumptions on both sides, and chasms in experience, which decisively divided them. Not surprisingly, the world of the busy academic was remote from the concerns of a lonely and aspirant fifteen-year-old in Umtata. For Lily, still living in a world in which misfortune was explained in terms of individual wickedness and witchcraft, Mabel's failure to reply could only be the result of the evil counsel of her advisers. Equally, however, Lily's Anglican milieu of the Eastern Cape was as remote to the secular, Fabian vision of a Mabel Palmer. For Mabel, Lily's intense if adolescent religious experience was to appear as 'religiosity' and 'self-righteous', while she had difficulty initially remembering whether her 'protegée' was an Anglican or a Catholic, and no idea that she was Xhosa, not Zulu.[51] These divisions had no place in the 'rational' modernism Fabians espoused.

IV

By the middle of 1950 Mabel had determined to send Lily to Adams College, the famous African high-school in Natal. There was much logic in her choice. She knew the staff of the school through the numerous winter schools she had organised there, and she approved its interdenominationalism. The oldest educational establishment in Natal, Adams had a reputation as a pioneering African high school, 'a haven of comparative freedom in a strange land'.[52] Founded as the Amanzimtoti Institute in 1853 by the American Board of Missions and renamed in the 1930s after its pioneer medical missionary, Dr Newton Adams, the school was intended from the outset to train teachers and ministers and to cater for those 'capable of profiting from a course of studies beyond that provided in the normal day school'.[53] Nevertheless some fifty years later, the average enrolment was only 41 boys, with less than a quarter going beyond Standard VI. By the mid-twentieth century, student numbers had risen to about 500, and the school had been fully co-educational for more than forty years, taking boys and girls to matriculation standard. Adams at that time consisted of a secondary school, a teacher training college and an industrial department in which youths were taught woodwork and building skills. Most of the students were in their late teens and early twenties.

Co-education and the fact that it was the first college in Natal to give responsible posts to African teachers gave the institution its progressive image. Among the first of these African teachers were Chief Albert Luthuli, later President of the African National Congress and Nobel prize-winner, and Z. K. Matthews, who was appointed headmaster of the High School in 1925 over black and white staff.[54] Like Chief Luthuli, Dr Matthews was to become prominent in Congress politics in the 1950s, and stood trial for treason with him in 1956. Before that he had had an outstanding academic career, as Lecturer in Social Anthropology and African Government and Law at the University College of Fort Hare in 1937, and Professor of African Studies and Head of Department there in 1945. Earlier hopes that Adams would become the African constituent of a multi-racial University of Natal had not been realised, but it

19

ran a teachers' training college recognised by the Natal Department of Education.[55]

In 1940, the American Board 'handed over the College, lock, stock and barrel, to a Board of Governors, the majority of whose members were South Africans and of varied religious persuasions'. Nevertheless, close co-operation with the mission continued and the 'distinctly religious foundation and character of the College' remained in the forefront of its new constitution: Adams College was to continue 'in perpetuity as a Christian educational institution for the Bantu people of South Africa and adjacent territories'.[56] Although the vast majority of students were drawn from the Christian African elite of Natal, who could manage to keep their children at school beyond the primary standards and could afford the school fees, a trickle of students did indeed make their way to Adams from the rest of South Africa and the 'adjacent territories', from as far afield as Kenya, Uganda and Tanzania.

The careers open to Africans in South Africa in the mid-century were few and far between, but most of the matriculants — simply because the numbers who reached that stage were also few and far between — would go on to form part of the small but distinguished African intelligentsia and professional class of twentieth century South Africa — teachers, ministers, doctors, nurses, lawyers and writers.[57] Mabel was not being unrealistic when she mused on the possibilities for her 'little protegée' of becoming a teacher, nurse, health assistant, or even training as a doctor at the newly opened black medical school: with a matriculation certificate, Lily would have been one of a minute number of black women to reach that level of education, and many of the obstacles in the way of a career would have indeed been overcome, as she herself realised.

In September 1950, even before she had received the necessary documentation from the school, Lily ran away to Adams, where Mabel Palmer had promised to support her. After an exciting journey, she managed to find her way to the school. 'Jack' Grant, who became Principal of Adams at the beginning of 1949, described it as Lily, with her previous experience of the more imposing Anglican architecture of St John's College, Umtata, may have seen it:

20

To one who visits the College for the first time a disappointment may be in store. For, instead of seeing an orderly arrangement of buildings, one will see little more than a wooded hilly expanse of some 600 acres. Closer inspection will reveal class-room accommodation, dormitories, a kitchen and dining hall, workshops, homes, vegetable gardens, cane-fields, pasturage, playing fields, reservoirs and other such amentiies inseparable from a large boarding establishment.[58]

Whatever her impressions of the school, Lily was relieved to have left Umtata. As she put it to Mabel in a letter on the 7th September, at home 'things were becoming worse, unbearable and torturous'. Some days later she explained more fully:

The climax if not reached, was about to be reached. Besides all the other reasons I once gave you before, all along our long correspondence I had never told you this and now I feel compelled to tell you that I could, or in fact [would] try to endure every other difficulty patiently and humbly, but not to see myself getting married in an awkward manner to a man I hated so much. That is one of the things I so much hate being married. I don't even dream about it. That awful bondage. That is what my uncle did to me . . .[59]

Mission records of the nineteenth and early twentieth centuries are replete with stories of women fleeing to the stations to escape an unwelcome marriage. Central to the political economy of precolonial African society was the control which the homestead head, whether father, uncle, husband or guardian, had over women. Women were exchanged against cattle, *lobolo* or bride-wealth, an exchange of cattle between men for the productive and reproductive powers of women. Despite the opposition of missionaries, who saw *lobolo* as the 'sale' of women, the practice persisted, although in the twentieth century it came to represent the redistribution of resources between families rather than an exchange of cattle for present and future labour power.[60] The persistence of *lobolo*, bolstered by the South African state, gave continued power of male guardians over African women,

21

who, unless specifically exempted from the provisions of customary law (and very few were), were regarded as perpetual minors. As the African educator, the Revd John Dube, himself no simple-minded advocate of European mission values, put it in 1925:

> The women who respond more quickly to the preaching of the Gospel are confronted with the difficulties of lobola. This custom is a great hindrance to the spread of the Gospel. So long as our women are looked upon as an asset of commercial value, so long will the progress of the Native be retarded. . . .[61]

In the straitened circumstances of Lily's family, it seems her uncle hoped to enrich himself by marrying her off for the bridewealth. For Lily, this was the last straw. Fiercely resenting her dependence, she had no desire to be married, least of all to a man of her uncle's choice.

In Lily's case — and perhaps, too, in Sibusisiwe Makhanya's, as we shall see — there may have been an additional element in the rejection of marriage: the desire of the ambitious and clever woman to distance herself from the 'frivolity' of peer group preoccupations with courting and marriage. For an African woman determined to carve out her own career, moreover, the demands of domesticity imposed serious obstacles. Above all, however, for the serious-minded and adolescent Lily the teachings of the Anglican church, and in particular its emphasis on sexual purity, appear to have made an indelible impression.

Central to the identity of the Christian elite of the Eastern Cape were the high educational standards they set themselves, a demanding ideology of respectability and a tightly puritanical sexual code. Much of this was common to mission converts in general, a reflection of the middle-class evangelism which had attempted to change working class morality, transposed to Africa. And as amongst 'labour aristocracy' in Britain, so amongst the African petty bourgeoisie, the pursuit of respectability was 'an assertion of social superiority, a self-conscious cultural exclusion of less favoured groups'.[62] The construction of an alternative sexual code was of particular importance perhaps to the Anglicans of Tsolo district. From the very beginning, the missionaries at St Cuthbert's had been concerned with 'the question of purity': Bransby Key had considered it a 'burning question' in 1883, and planned 'to start a guild for the promotion of purity among the girls'.[63]

This was perhaps no more than the stock Victorian missionary response to African nudity, female initiation rites, and openness about sex. Nevertheless, the fact that St Cuthbert's Mission was placed in the hands of the celibate brotherhood of the Society of St John the Evangelist may have reinforced this preoccupation with African sexuality in church teaching in the Tsolo district. By the beginning of the twentieth century, a sisterhood had been formed at St Cuthbert's, and the first black nun confirmed. 'A spinning wheel and the knowledge of how to use it' were seen as most useful in filling the 'somewhat dangerous time between the completion of a girl's schooling and her marriage'.[64]

Concern with the virginity of young African girls remained a recurrent theme amongst missionaries, administrators and Christian Africans in twentieth century South Africa. It lay behind the repeated fears expressed by African men and colonial administrators of the temptations in the way of young girls in towns, the formation of mothers' prayer unions or *manyanos* by African women in the mission churches as early as 1912, the establishment of hostels for unmarried women in Johannesburg and Durban by missionaries of the American Board, and the organisation of the Bantu Purity League in 1919 by Sibusisiwe Makhanya.[65]

There were material foundations to these fears. By the beginning of the twentieth century, changed patterns of child-rearing threw the burden of sex education on mothers rather than on grandmothers and peer-group as in the past: the result of mission abhorrence of female initiation ceremonies and the development of the nuclear family, especially amongst Christian Africans. The migrant labour system which deprived the villages of young men and put great pressures on the girls on their return exacerbated these problems at a time when safe forms of external sexual intercourse were either forgotten or frowned on by the church. At the same time, town, mission station and colonial employment opened up opportunities to women who wished to escape unwelcome marriage partners and the constraints of a gerontocratic and patriarchal order. Both their potential independence and their vulnerability aroused a passionate response. In town and countryside, the rate of premarital pregnancy was high and the concern with adolescent 'purity' intense. Colonial fears of miscegenation further fanned by the eugenicist ideas of the time articulated with the concerns of African men that their women were a prey to men of other races and that they were losing control over 'their' women and youth.

Problems of sexual 'purity' and identity run as a *leitmotiv* through the history of the three women in this correspondence: a reflection of the dominated and distorted nature of sexual relations for both black and white women in the twentieth century. For Mabel, the 'problems of celibacy for university women' in early twentieth century Britain, and the absence of any true sexual equality were a major concern; the lives of both Sibusisiwe Makhanya and Lily were dramatically shaped by the patriarchy of their own society and its disruptions by an equally, if very different, patriarchal mission Christianity and the form of South Africa's racially structured capitalist order, based on a migrant labour system.[66] Structural preconditions do not, of course, explain personal psychology. The delicate chemistry between the individual and his or her social context can never be reduced simply to that social context. At the same time, however, individual psychology is a profoundly historical phenomenon, the product of the multiple determinations which in the final analysis shape the forms and meanings of experience.

For Lily, the particularities of Christian Xhosa patriarchy and the construction of sexuality in the Anglican milieu of the Eastern Cape were inescapable; anxiety about 'purity' and her own adolescent sexuality, permeate the correspondence. This we have already seen in the letter she wrote Mabel in response to her requests for an account of life in the 'native reserves', and the fears of marriage which were the final precipitant in her running away from home in September 1950. Problems with the opposite sex were to continue to plague Lily even at Adams, and were amongst the reasons for her increasing unhappiness at the school. Despite the fact that her report at the end of her first term at Adams suggested to the principal 'a satisfactory beginning', almost from the outset there were signs that she attracted attention and teasing.[67]

24

By June 1951, she was complaining to Mabel that she had 'lost pride of and appetite on Adams', and that its coeducation was 'abominable'. At the end of an exceptionally bitter diatribe against the indiscipline, lack of morality and 'education which is barbarism[68] under a camouflage' at Adams, Lily added

> P.S. and I have never come across such raw school-boys as Adams students who have no respect who force and say anything they like to girls. . . . I can be very glad if I can go to a school with no boys what-so-ever.[69]

We cannot know precisely what lay behind Lily's outspoken antipathy towards the 'raw schoolboys' at Adams in June 1951. The pressures can only be guessed at from her fleeting remarks. Some further idea, however, of the extent of the problem can be guaged from the records of the American Board of Missions in Natal. In 1940, for example, the famous girls' school at Inanda, the sister school to Adams, experienced the 'loss' in one week of two unmarried teachers and two students as a result of pregnancy; in the following year seven girl students, four of them new and including one of fifteen who subsequently died, presumably in childbirth, were sent down as a result of 'moral failure'.[70]

The problem was not confined to students. In 1946 an African teacher was dismissed from Adams, 'because of serious indiscretions in his conduct with one of the girl students' and anecdotal evidence suggests that this was more widespread.[71] It is difficult to find statistics of sexual 'misdemeanours' for Adams for the year that Lily was there, but the problems for an inexperienced, new teenage girl at a coeducational school, at which the number of boys considerably outnumbered the number of girls, were likely to have been intense. Given her fears of being married off for the bridewealth which precipitated her flight to Natal and hint at a very real threat of coercion, her 'curious antipathy to boys and men', is more than explicable.[72] In the light of the nature of social relations at this time, there is certainly some evidence for thinking that Lily may have been subjected to fairly violent sexual advances, which she could not handle.

25

V

A dislike of 'raw school-boys' was certainly not the only reason for Lily's unhappiness at Adams, however. Absolom Vilakazi, the noted African anthropologist, has remarked on the degree of control which the Church and its teaching have exerted over Christian Africans. The Church, he argues

> has taken the place of the kinship group for most Christians, and its systems of dependence which support the individual are as important for the Christians as the kinship systems of reciprocity and mutuality to the traditionalists. To transgress the canons of the Church, therefore, is for the Christian similar to breaking the family or kinship customary practices. Both have the effect of invoking the sanction which, in each case is the withdrawal of support and customary reciprocities.[73]

For the devout Lily, whose entire life had been bound up with the Anglican church and its schools, the transition to the interdenominational Adams clearly transgressed highly significant boundaries. Her experience of the Anglican schools with their high academic standards and their sense of order and decorum may also have lain behind her bitter disappointment with the more democratic and open Adams tradition. The difference between the Cape Anglican schools with their stress on a common academic standard for black and white, and the Natal educational system added to these tensions.

In the first half of this century, Natal's schools for Africans were heavily influenced by the American educational and race relations nexus constituted by corporate philanthropy. Natal educationalists visiting the United States of America entered a network which took them to Thomas Jesse Jones, the pioneer race relations 'expert' at the Phelps-Stokes Foundation in New York, the American Board of Missions based in Boston, Hampton, the first all-black college in the United States, and Tuskegee, the famous industrial school founded by the ex-slave, Booker T. Washington in Alabama in 1878. The objectives of Tuskegee, to inculcate notions of self-help, manual labour and interracial co-operation amongst emancipated blacks in the

American South, were seen as particularly appropriate for colonial Africa. The American educational philosophy which aimed to 'train blacks sufficiently for life in a modern society yet served to limit any challenge they might pose to white control', was transmitted to Natal largely through the instrumentality of the missionaries of the American Zulu Mission (as the American Board was known in Natal) and the influential Natal educationalist and 'expert' on 'race relations', C.T. Loram.[74] The result was a system in which hygiene and agriculture, needlework and domestic science, were considered far more important than algebra or geometry, in contrast with the allegedly 'academic' and 'bookish' education in the Cape.[75]

It is impossible to know with any certainty what these differences actually meant in daily practice in the mid-century, or how they would have been experienced by Lily. Already noted as 'difficult' by her mentors in Umtata, she was clearly dissatisfied with what she perceived as the low academic standards as well as the absence of order at Adams, and the authoritarianism of one of her teachers.[76] Although her denunciation of the school led Mabel to view Lily as self-centred and unbalanced, her views are to a considerable extent substantiated both by the matriculation results at Adams and by the recollections of the distinguished African writer, Eskia ('Zik) Mphahlele, who attended Adams a few years earlier and who also went there from an Anglican high school, the well-known St Peter's in Sophiatown. In an interview with Chabani Manganyi, Mphahlele has recalled those years:

> When I got to Adams the first thing that hit me was, my word, I seemed to have come to a jungle in comparison with St Peter's. There was order in the dorms at St Peter's. There were standards of cleanliness, standards of hygiene. Not at Adam's. My, my, my. (*Laughter*) There you really had to survive. . . . All in all, the academic achievement of students wasn't anything to talk about. . . . Their matric results were very ordinary, mostly second and third classes . . . .[77]

In *Down Second Avenue*, his early autobiography, Mphahlele described Adams as 'more like a mine compound', than a school.

27

Nor were lack of order and low educational standards all that concerned Mphahlele during his years at Natal:

> I left Adams with a nagging feeling of a strong memory of tribalism that prevailed in Natal. . . . The province is Zulu country and the bulk of the students at Adams had always been Zulus. They did not like non-Zulu boys and girls coming to the college. They regarded us as foreigners.[78]

Despite its distinguished past,[79] the Adams to which Lily came in the late 1940s was not a happy place. In 1947 an unpopular principal had been forced to resign after two unexplained cases of arson, a threatening letter and a student boycott of the examinations. Edgar Brookes, a former principal, wrote as an insider of 'chaos, distrust and almost despair'.[80] Although the previous somewhat weak principal had been replaced by the experienced and able G.C. Grant, the trouble continued and during Lily's very first fortnight at the college, 175 students were sent home for failing to attend chapel. The immediate cause of the upheavel was Grant's refusal to allow the Zulu Society to hold a dance to commemorate Shaka Day, on the grounds that it 'tended to arouse intertribal conflict'. Grant was sensitive to the issue, for in June that year he had expelled two Zulu students who had 'waylaid' and assaulted a Xhosa student, an incident he attributed to 'a little flare-up of intertribal tension'.[81]

Although at Adams the discontent took this particular ethnic form, it was part of the very widespread disaffection in African high schools after World War II which, like the formation of the African National Congress Youth League, reflected the new political mood among Africans.[82] It was the increased self-assertiveness amongst graduates of the mission schools which in part fuelled Nationalist determination to restructure African education. After the disturbances, Adams, like other mission boarding schools, faced a vicious onslaught by the Nationalist government which eventually took it over in 1956. In the tense and unpleasant situation in September 1950, it is perhaps not entirely surprising that Lily found it difficult to settle down. Mabel was soon to express concern at her inability to form friendships with her fellow-students, who even accused her of being a spy, and to stress the importance of her making friends amongst her 'own', i.e. black, people. Vulnerable, insecure and an alien Xhosa amongst the majority of Zulu-speaking students — an aspect of the situation to which Mabel remained oblivious — Lily became increasingly dependent on her relationship with her white surrogate guardian, increasingly desperate for emotional support. By the beginning of 1951, she had had enough of Adams and wanted to finish her matriculation studies in Durban, in order as she put it to Mabel, to 'be in touch with your school, your people and with many other civilized branches [of education]'.[83]

Mabel's response was swift and sharp. In a long letter, cataloguing Lily's various misdemeanours, she proceeded to make her position very clear. The letter is worth quoting at length, both for what it reveals of Mabel and its significance in Lily's life:

> You say that among your reasons for wishing to be in Durban is that you want to see more of me, but have you ever asked yourself whether I wish to see more of you? As a matter fact I do not. Your romantic and self-centred imagination has built up for you a picture in which you are to be my devoted and intimate friend. Now you must forgive me for saying that this is all nonsense. Even if you were a European girl of your age it would still be nonsense. What basis of companionship could there be between a quarter educated girl of eighteen and an experienced old lady like myself? And of course the racial situation in Durban makes all these things more difficult. . . .
>
> You say you want to help me. The best way that you can help me is by staying at Adams and doing as well as you can both in your work and getting on with the other students, and that would be the best return you can make for the kindness I am showing you. That kindness does not necessarily involve any personal or intimate friendship. Indeed such an intimate friendship is impossible and could only be achieved on the basis of equal interest and experience which does not exist between you and me.
>
> Mrs Bernard Shaw, long ago, gave me a scholarship

which she paid out of her own pocket in order that I might go and study in America. I did not for that reason expect to become her intimate friend. I wrote her a letter of thanks and then waited for her to make the next move. When she made no move whatever and I did not meet her at all until very much later, I did not feel that I had any grievance. The way in which you must pay me back is the way in which I am paying back Mrs Bernard Shaw, namely by extending help to another poor and ambitious student many years later when in a position to do so.[84]

This letter marked a turning point in Lily's sojourn at Adams. Despite a duly submissive reply, from this time her work began to deteriorate — from a position of 13th in a class of 22 in December 1950 she dropped to 20th in a class of 28 by June — and she began to complain of 'rhuematism' [sic], and then depression.[85] Although her demands on Mabel for emotional support seem to have diminished, in May 1951 she requested permission to visit her family in Johannesburg. When the school refused to grant this — fearful lest the visit place her once more in her guardian's power — Lily's behaviour began to rouse angry comment from the newly appointed Dean of Women Students, apparently a stern disciplinarian who had recently arrived from Germany.[86] Two letters from Lily to Mabel at the beginning of June suggest that by this time the former was paranoid and distraught. Mabel read them as evidence of her 'maladjustment', while Sibusisiwe Makhanya thought that Lily's behaviour and accusations against an African male teacher were the result of an illegitimate pregnancy, a diagnosis which was probably incorrect, but is revealing both of Sibusisiwe's preoccupations and of sexual mores at the time.[87]

VI

It was Mabel's inability to handle Lily's isolation and demands for emotional support which brought Sibusisiwe or Violet Makhanya into her story. To some extent, Sibusisiwe represents a crucial bridge between the 'separate worlds' of the title. Like Lily, she was the daughter of Christian parents, this time converts of the Congregationalist American Board, who never-theless 'saw no incongruity in observing many of the old Zulu traditions'.[88] By the time she was born, her father, who had worked in the Durban docks as a labourer, was a successful 'progressive' farmer, with a plough, wagons and mules, producing vegetables and maize for the local market. Her maternal kinsman, the Revd John Dube, was probably the best-known black educationalist and political leader in early twentieth-century Natal. Sibusisiwe was born in 1894. Educated at the American Board's girls' school, Inanda — where she was almost expelled for not being 'quiet and well-behaved like the other girls' — and later at the Teachers' College at Adams, then known as the Amanzimtoti Institute, she herself became a teacher at Inanda Seminary. Clearly she had redeemed her earlier reputation for naughtiness.

Described as 'the outstanding Zulu woman of her generation', 'a living answer to the question "Why missions?" ', she seemed to epitomise the American 'adaptionist' model of education in Natal, although, as we shall see, the reality was more complex.[89] Despite much local opposition to her activities which were regarded as unseemly for a Zulu woman, her powerful person-ality and secure parental background, the strength and coherence of her Zulu identity and the nature of the American Zulu Mission ensured that she never suffered the alienation so evident in Lily's correspondence. Her extensive interviews with her American biographer, Myrtle Trowbridge, reveal a powerful and confident personality, nurtured by a warm and loving family, in which a sense of community with both her Christian and non-Christian neighbours and kin were encouraged from an early age. Unlike Lily, Sibusisiwe never became a 'victim', and for this reason too her responses to her situation are instructive.

Even as a young woman, Sibusisiwe, or, as she was better known in mission circles at that time, Violet, had taken an interest in community affairs, and by the early 1920s had started an organisation called the Bantu Purity League, in order to improve the 'moral standards' of African girls. As Bertha Mkize put it subsequently, the League aimed 'to keep the girls pure in the right way' — at a time when, as we have seen, the extent of premarital pregnancy, especially amongst Christian girls, was causing considerable alarm in black and white mission circles.[90]

31

Sibusisiwe's work both in the Bantu Purity League and in running a night school from her home at Umbumbulu much impressed both the Phelps-Stokes Commission on Education in East and Southern Africa when they visited Natal in the 1920s, and C.T. Loram, the ex-Natal Inspector of Schools and then member of the Native Affairs Commission, who accompanied them.[91] As a result, in 1927 she was offered a scholarship, sponsored by the South African government but actually granted by the Phelps-Stokes Fund in New York, to train as a Jeanes teacher in the United States of America.[92] Like Lily, at a later date, however, Sibusisiwe very rapidly established herself as 'a difficult pupil'. Already in her thirties, independent-minded and articulate, she refused to be shaped by the philanthropic intentions of the Phelps-Stokes network into accepting permanent white supremacy. Within a few months, she had rebelled against both the teaching at Penn School, South Carolina, which was the model of Jeanes training chosen for Africans, and the ten-week summer school she attended at Tuskegee. Like a number of Africans brought to the United States by the Phelps-Stokes Fund at this time, she found the training offered irrelevant to her needs. Neither Penn School nor Tuskegee offered the general theoretical background to social work deemed necessary for white students at that time.[93]

Breaking her ties with the Phelps-Stokes Fund and thus with her financial supporters, Sibusisiwe made her way first to the Schauffler Institute for Social and Theological Training in Cleveland (which merged with the famous Congregationalist school of theology at Oberlin in 1954), and then to the Teachers College, Columbia University, the mecca of Africans disaffected with the Phelps-Stokes/Tuskegee-Hampton system of education. Clearly, she was aware that the rurally based educational system of the black South was no longer applicable to the rapidly changing social situation of Africans in South Africa, undergoing the strains of intensive industrialisation and proletarianisation. In New York, she encountered Mabel Carney, 'a pioneer in the field of black and rural education', who had visited Natal in 1926.[94]

The relationship between the two women was very different to that established by Lily with Mabel Palmer, although it does seem as though, in the very early days, Sibusisiwe misjudged the relationship of teacher and pupil in a busy metropolitan college.

Thus according to her biographer,

> Anxious to learn all she could, she was not only raising
> many questions in class, but was constantly consulting
> Miss Carney. She found the street, and number where her
> teacher lived. Somewhat frightened, she rang the door
> bell. She was graciously received. . . . With such encourage-
> ment, she failed to realize how often she was ringing the
> bell. One morning after some delay Miss Carney opened
> the door. She was in her bathrobe. As gently as she could,
> she told Sibusisiwe that she must quit coming to the house
> unless she was in dire need. She went on to explain that
> she had but one refuge from her work, and that she must
> not be interrupted at such inconvenient hours.[95]

Mortified, Sibusisiwe rushed home and wept. The next day
she asked Miss Carney's forgiveness. 'From that moment, she
had no stauncher friend.'[96] Mabel Carney became one of
Sibusisiwe's enthusiastic supporters and acted as secretary of a
group of American philanthropists who assisted Sibusisiwe
financially on her return to South Africa in 1930.[97]

Back in South Africa, Sibusisiwe re-established herself at
Umbumbulu, in the heart of the Umlazi district, homeland of
the Makhanya people. Here Christianity had a long history —
the Umlazi mission was one of the earliest in Natal, having been
granted to the American Board in 1836. Nevertheless, most of
her relatives and neighbours were pagan. As D.H. Reader, the
anthropologist who worked from Sibusisiwe's centre and
dedicated his study of the Makhanya people to 'Sibusisiwe,
Leader of her People', saw it in 1951, 'Christian and pagans'
were 'intermixed in the same total community, and their modes
of life are not encapsulated, but polarities joined in a con-
tinuum'.[98] In a sense this was crucial to Sibusisiwe's understanding of her task.

If the Makhanya people had been long exposed to Christianity, they had also been long exposed to the colonial political
economy. By the 1930s the majority were dependent on labour
migration to Durban to support their way of life. The 'traditional'
way of life, although far from disintegrating, was no longer
self-sufficient in the face of the demands being made upon it.[99]

For Sibusisiwe and her generation the key to coping with the pressures of capitalist development was 'adaptation' to westernization and education. This did not mean jettisoning all the old ways: and as she grew older, Sibusisiwe saw greater value in 'tradition', But it did mean absorbing 'foreign social institutions' and making them compatible with indigenous ones'.[100] With this end in view, on her return to Umbumbulu, Sibusisiwe organised a new youth movement entitled the Bantu Youth League under the chairmanship of the Revd John Dube. Its objects were

1 To nurture in Bantu youths the ideals of good citizenship as exemplified in the life of Christ.
2 To encourage . . . self-confidence in Bantu youths by the preservation of constructive ideals and customs of the Zulu people.
3 To encourage co-operation among native youth leaders.
4 To break down sectarianism.
5 To cultivate appreciation of the culture of other races and to encourage interracial co-operation.[101]

Or, as the missionary and headmistress of Inanda, Lavinia Scott, succintly put it, 'to promote right ideals and wholesome interests among the young people of her nation'.[102] At Umbumbulu, Sibusisiwe created a social centre and school from which in effect she carried out many of the central precepts of Jeanes — and Loram's — teaching.

Thus, just about the time that Sibusisiwe had left for the States, Loram had written of the 'Native school building [acting as] . . . the centre of the whole new life of the community':

Here should be the headquarters of the Native Farmers' Association, the Village Library, the Boy Scout and Girl Guide Movements, the Mothers' Union, the Choral Society, Home Demonstrators and the rest of the uplifting force in the community.[103]

Perhaps more influenced by Mabel Carney's teaching than Penn School or Tuskegee, this was very much the model which Sibusisiwe followed at Umbumbulu. In 1934 on the occasion of

34

her second visit to South Africa, Mabel Carney described her as:

> the energetic Zulu girl who studied in our department
> during the spring of 1930 . . . Miss Makhanya is director
> of the Bantu Youth League, an organisation similar to the
> YWCA which she originated several years ago and which
> now enrolls some 600 young people with 25 branches
> scattered over Natal. Her activities include work for both
> adolescents and adults centering around a community
> house built under her direct supervision, even to the
> making of the cement blocks. Unquestionably she is highly
> regarded in South Africa by both her colleagues and the
> Native people. . . .[104]

Her 'regular community activities [which] included a demonstration garden, a winter school for girls and women and Sunday school . . . an annual leadership conference for community workers . . . and a night school for herder boys',[105] were very close in fact to Loram's concepts. Indeed after seeing her work in Natal during his African tour of 1932–3, Dr Stokes recommended that the Fund support the Bantu Youth League to the tune of $50 to $100.[106] She had clearly redeemed herself in the eyes of philanthropic capital.

As her earlier defiance of the Phelps-Stokes Fund showed, however, Sibusisiwe was a woman of spirit and independence which led her to a strongly developed sense of what was known at the time as 'race consciousness'. During her sojourn in the United States, for example, she continued to send donations to the Industrial and Commercial Workers' Union and kept in touch with its fiery, populist, nationalist leader, A.W.G. Champion, whom we have already encountered in his confrontation with Mabel Palmer. Amongst the reasons for her discontent with the Phelps-Stokes Fund was the refusal of its officers to consult with her and give her a proper hearing, and it may have been in response to her complaints about this that Champion wrote to her at the end of 1929:

> My dear Sibusisiwe our people are oppressed as a race and
> they are oppressed by those who employ them, having no
> voice whatsoever in the management of their affairs. . . .

May I hope that the seed that lies in the breast of all human beings, seeds of race consciousness, will find enough moisture in the USA and let you, our daughter, come back to Africa prepared to continue the struggle for Africa's liberation. When we speak of Africa's liberation we do not say Europeans must leave Africa, but we say let the Africans enjoy equal opportunities with Europeans and let there be no discrimination. . . .[107]

There is little doubt that Sibusisiwe found the 'seeds of race consciousness' in the 'moisture' of the United States and was influenced by the sense of 'race pride' so much in evidence amongst black Americans in the inter-war period. Thus, after a meeting with Dr Robert Moton, the Principal of Tuskegee, at friends in New York, she wrote asking if he could introduce her to one or two people who would be interested in her proposed social work in South Africa:

It would mean so much to me to have one or two introductions arranged for me by an outstanding member of my own race as well as by members of the white race. Above everything else I crave for my work in Africa the interest and support of my own people in America. I do not feel that it is enough to have merely the support and interest of white people. Whatever you as an individual or Tuskegee as a whole can do for the young people of South Africa will be appreciated to an extent difficult for me to put into words.[108]

As the above correspondence and Sibusisiwe's somewhat 'turbulent' career in the United States indicates, she was no mere acceptor of white middle-class values. Nor, unlike Lily, had she been cut off from her community as a result of her Christian upbringing and mission education. She was closely connected to the chiefly rulers of the Makhanya people, and although her kinsmen disapproved of her activities and particularly of her going overseas, they came to accept her exceptional position. Sibusisiwe's concern with purity arose out of her own and her class's deeply felt experience, and resonated with the views of the traditional hierarchy. Her race consciousness was equally part of that deep experience, transmuted in the 1930s into an ethnic, cultural nationalism.[109] By the second half of the thirties, she was one of the 'advisers' of the Zulu Society, amongst whose aims was the adaptation of the Zulu to contemporary society while maintaining the best of 'traditional' life — the indiscipline of the young and the breakdown of male control over women was at the heart of the organisation's concerns. In keeping with this return to 'traditionalism', she broke her ties with the teetotal American Board, apparently because on her return from the States she began the brewing and sale of *utshwala* (African millet beer) at Umbumbulu. Her kinsman, the School Inspector, H. M. S. Makhanya recalled years later how Sibusisiwe returned from America 'different', regarding beerbrewing simply as a 'useful trade':

> I remember the year she was excommunicated from the church because the people regarded one intelligent enough has no business to participate in anything that has got to do with beer. Oh, she thought it was nothing . . . when she came back drinking was nothing and she sold beer herself. She started a beerhall here, not far away from her place . . . churches overseas don't ban alcoholic drinks.[110]

At the same time, because of her emphasis on 'welfare' rather than 'politics', Sibusisiwe remained a shining example for whites of what an African woman could achieve within the limits of the segregationist and patriarchal social system, through 'adaptation'. Edgar Brookes, for example, described her as 'a great social worker . . . [who] combined a very modern social conscience with a respect for the old tribal institutions'.[111]

When Lily met her, then, at the beginning of 1950, Sibusisiwe had a formidable reputation amongst her circle as a community worker. Visitors, especially American visitors flocked to the centre to meet her, and were always assured of a warm and friendly welcome. Unusually for that time and place, Sibusisiwe was able to accommodate white missionaries and scholars studying Zulu and the Zulu people in the home she herself had built on land given her by her father. Her experiences in the United States gave her an assurance and confidence in dealing with whites from a position of equality which were

37

also rare in the first half of this century.

By the time Lily came to Adams, Sibusisiwe had very close connections with the school, even sitting on the sub-committee to choose the new principal in 1947.[112] In that year, she continued her school for herdboys, organised adult education classes with voluntary teachers and ran a small library and clinic at Umbumbulu which became an inter-racial centre. It was at Umbumbulu that Lily spent her vacations and occasional weekends, and from Umbumbulu that she eventually fled from Natal.

There is no evidence as to when and where Mabel and Sibusisiwe first met, although their common connection with Adams in the 1930s suggests it may have been there. In 1931, they both gave evidence to the Native Economic Commission, although their approach was very different. Both, it is true, were concerned with education and community work, but Mabel's emphasis was decidedly intellectual and political, Sibusisiwe's domestic and social. As Sibusisiwe put it in a report to her American sponsors in 1935, 'Our general aim may be summed up in the slogan, "Better homes for better Africans".[113] In their contrasting social contexts, however, they would both have seen themselves as fighting for the goal of 'liberating' women through education, though the conception of what this entailed for Mabel, coming from her British suffragette and Fabian background and Sibusisiwe, product of American evangelism and Zulu heritage, was necessarily very different. For Mabel, the lack of sexual freedom for women in Victorian England had been a central preoccupation in the years before World War I; for Sibusisiwe, the breakdown of African family life and therefore the need to control adolescent sexuality and to substitute for women's old roles a new domesticity were far more crucial than personal sexual fulfilment.[114] The differences are illuminated perhaps by the nature of the summer schools which Mabel devised for the Fabian Society for recreational and political pursuits and the winter schools which Sibusisiwe ran for women and girls, who were taught 'knitting, gardening, sewing, house-work, cookery, native craft work, tree planting'.[115]

Whatever their differences, and the wholly different contexts in which they operated, by the late 1940s, their relationship seems to have been based on affection and mutual regard. Both were dedicated to education and both were forceful and effective single women. Despite a number of serious relationships with men, at the age of twenty-six Sibusisiwe deliberately decided not to marry in order to carry on her life-work.[116] As H.M.S. Makhanya remarked in 1979:

> I know why she didn't get married. You know amongst our people a woman has got to be very nice and humble. She wasn't. She was so outspoken. She would come here and talk to [older] men and women as she would to her friends and the young men regarded her with fear. [Young men say] 'I can't live with such a woman — she's a boss to me.'[117]

Mabel's 'assertive commonsense' was perhaps matched by Sibusisiwe's 'outspokenness'. As Lily was to remark of her: 'What I most like of her she is not a hypocrite.'[118]

VII

By the beginning of November 1950, Mabel was writing to Sibusisiwe to help her with Lily who was turning out to be more difficult than the older woman in her enthusiasm had anticipated. 'Completely cut off ... from her own people', Lily needed 'some contact with Bantu friends outside Adams College.' As a 'woman of her own race', Mabel thought Sibusisiwe might be able to help Lily think 'more effectively ... more of other people and less of herself'; over the next few months, the young Lily spent her weekends at Umbumbulu. She described herself as always feeling 'at home' with Sibusisiwe, or as she put it 'homely'.[119] In June 1951 Mabel sent Sibusisiwe Lily's outburst against Adams; as a member of the Council, she felt Sibusisiwe 'may like to consider whether there is any fragment of truth in Lily's charges'.[120]

Clearly, then, Mabel expected Sibusisiwe to straddle the 'separate worlds' of the white woman academic, Fabian philanthropist, and the world of the young Christian girl. Whether Sibusisiwe was really in a better position to empathize with the by now desperately lonely and vulnerable adolescent, given her Zulu Congregationalist background, community activities and personal forcefulness, is less clear. By the beginning of June she too was becoming impatient with the intractable and friendless Lily.[121]

Concerned at her unhappiness, if uncomprehending, Mabel, generous as ever, determined to give Lily a last chance. Energetically, she explored the possibilities of enrolling her for the following session either in the Girls' School at Inanda or at the Catholic St Francis College and High School at Mariannhill, where Mabel assumed that they 'keep the boys and girls rather carefully separate'.[122] Although the syllabus would have been broadly the same for the state-set matriculation examination, it is likely that at St Francis Lily would have experienced rather greater discipline than at Adams. Whether she would have been any happier is a moot point. The rivalry between Catholic and Protestant schools in Natal was considerable, and they had very different attitudes towards authority. While the Protestants were thought of as being independent and critical, Catholics were thought of as more dependent and submissive; while Africans identified Protestant churches with 'progress', the Catholic churches had a reputation of inculcating ideals of obedience both to their immediate mentors and to the demands of the Church. Among Africans it was believed that 'Whereas the Protestant English-speaking churches taught reading and writing and deliberately civilized or westernized, the Catholics taught their people how to "build and cultivate" '. And, until the emergence of the Black Consciousness Movement in the late 1960s which was associated in its earliest stages with graduates of Mariannhill like Steve Biko, there had been relatively few Catholic leaders in African society except within the confines of the Church itself.[123]

Again Mabel's act of generosity in finding Lily an alternative school was coupled with total emotional rejection, however. In a revealing phrase in her June outburst, Lily had written to Mabel that 'a parent or a guardian who . . . really wants [for] her daughter or adopted child fruitful results to his or her strenuous struggle in educating her, should place her under good influence'. For Mabel this once more went beyond the nature of the relationship she was willing to establish:

40

. . . in your letter you use the phrase 'adopted daughter'. I don't know if you were thinking of me and yourself when you used those words, but I feel I must make it plain that I do not and will not regard you in any such light and that I have never said anything to justify you in believing so. I was interested in your letters and sympathetic towards a girl struggling for better education, and I felt it was up to me to give you some help. That help I will give. . . . But what I want is that you should as soon as possible be in a position to stand on your own feet. Also as a rather forlorn little protegée I will from time to time see you for a talk and arrange for you small treats. . . . But beyond that I will not go and every time you press on me a desire for a more intimate relation you really force me back into reserve and guardedness in dealing with you . . . any close or intimate friendship between us is really not possible and will only spoil things if you grasp at it. But this doesn't mean that I am not interested in you or do not want to be kind to you; *I do* within due limits.

You talk a good deal of your prayers. Do you ever pray to be made more humble and less self-righteous, more adaptable and more sensible?[124]

The letter was harsh and unyielding. By this time arthritic, with poor sight and moving with great difficulty on account of her enormous girth,[125] Mabel sensed the limitations of what she could do for Lily. She was anxious that her 'rather forlorn little protegée' should 'stand on her own feet', as she herself had been forced to do as a young girl. For Lily this forthrightness came as final rejection. She responded with a bitter attack on Adams and a senior member of staff on 8th June. Although Mabel vigorously denounced Lily's accusations, they spurred her into even more careful enquiries on her behalf. By the end of June, Lily had left Adams under a cloud to spend the vacation with Sibusisiwe. She was clearly in unhappy and truculent mood, still anxious to go to visit her 'relatives' in Johannesburg. After further 'bad behaviour' at Umbumbulu, Lily once more sought resolution in flight: in the middle of July she left Sibusisiwe, ostensibly to visit Mabel in Durban, but she failed to appear.

Concerned, Mabel sought reassurance from the Manager of the Municipality's Native Affairs Department, who advised her 'not to be too disturbed' as Durban was 'full of Bantu girls who have run away from their guardians and most of them manage all right, get employment in factories and as domestic workers.'[126] On July 24th, Lily wrote short notes to Sibusisiwe and Mabel explaining that she was in Sophiatown and 'very ill'. She followed this with a longer letter to Mabel on the 26th:

> For congenial reasons I had to leave Adams, due to the fact that I was never meant to be a stone but a human being with feelings not either an experimental doll. . . .[127]

This was to be her last letter. Sibusisiwe consoled Mabel: 'Well. Dr Palmer, you did all you could for that girl but it seems it is difficult to find out what she really wants. . . .'[128] The love, support and attention Lily desperately craved were denied her to the end.

NOTES

1 For reasons which will become clear, I have used a pseudonym for the main characters who are still alive, or whose identification may cause discomfort to surviving relatives, though I have tried to remain true to the Victorian quality of their real Christian names. All the remaining characters have retained their original names. Some of the charm of this story lies in the old fashioned flavour of the names — Mabel, Violet, Alice. The name 'Lily' seemed particularly appropriate in the light of Sibusisiwe (Violet) Makhanya's remark in the course of a lecture on African women in 1936 that they were 'lilies of the veld in the homes, kraals and communities' (Papers of the Zulu Society, ZS Conferences, Natal Archives, Pietermaritzburg, Address to the Second Annual Conference, 1936). Even the name of Sibusisiwe's biographer has an appropriately Victorian ring — Myrtle.

2   L. Davidoff, 'Class and gender in Victorian England' in J. L. Newton,
    M. P. Ryan and J. R. Walkowitz, *Sex and Class in Women's History*,
    History Workshop series (London, 1983), 30.
3   See my *Ambiguities of Dependence: state, class and nationalism in
    early twentieth century Natal* (Baltimore and Johannesburg, 1986).
4   For a theoretical critique of what they regard as 'the implicit feminist
    assumption that there exists a commonality of interests and/or goals
    amongst all women' see Floya Anthias and Nira Yuval-Davis, 'Con-
    ceptualizing feminism — gender, ethnic and class divisions', *Feminist
    Review*, no. 15, November 1983, 62–75.
5   Details of Mabel's life are drawn from the biographical note by
    R. H. Burrows introducing her *The History of the Indians in Natal*
    (Natal Regional Survey, volume 10, Cape Town, 1957), and from
    her papers in the Killie Campbell Africana Library, University of
    Natal, Durban. Dr Sylvia Vietzen is currently writing a biography of
    Mabel Palmer.
6   This point is made by Burrows, p.vii.
7   Burrows, p.vii.
8   M. Cole, *The Story of Fabian Socialism* (London, 1961), 349. The
    Fabian Women's group was formed in 1908, in the face of con-
    siderable opposition from Beatrice Webb, with whom Mabel would
    appear to have been at loggerheads on a number of issues.
9   *Local Government in Scotland* (Edinburgh and London, 1904), 400.
10 There are today some 800,000 Indians in South Africa, most of
    them the descendants of indentured labour brought to work on
    Natal's sugar plantations in the second half of the 19th century.
    In 1957 Mabel Palmer published *The History of the Indians in Natal*,
    one of the first of such accounts to appear. She was also one of the
    main contributors to a meeting of the Council of the SAIRR held in
    Durban in January, 1965 on *The Indian as a South African* (pub-
    lished by the SAIRR, 1956). Mabel Palmer is still recalled with
    affection by her Indian ex-students in Natal. The overwhelming
    majority of Africans in Natal (including Zululand, some 4 million
    people today) speak Zulu and belong to the northern Nguni group of
    peoples; as we shall see, Mabel Palmer was far more ignorant of their
    history and culture. According to Sylvia Vietzen, Mabel had both her
    admirers and detractors. While some regarded her as a 'wonderful
    woman', 'Those who had to withstand her tenacity for a cause,
    especially men, in positions of authority, regarded her, quite natu-
    rally, as a menace'. ('Fabian Transplant: the Adams College Vacation
    Schools and the University, 1936–1952', paper presented to the
    Natal University Jubilee History Conference, July 1985, 7.)
11 This is based on oral information from her surviving friends, and
    especially the late Florence MacDonald, interviewed in Durban in

December 1982. S. Vietzen, 'Beyond school: some developments in higher education in Durban in the 1920s and the influence of Mabel Palmer' *(Natalia,* 14, 1984, 54—5) stresses Mabel Palmer's tremendous verve and versatility at this time. I am grateful to Ms M. P. Moberly for this reference.

12　Vietzen, 'Fabian Transplant', passim.

13　Ibid. 8.

14　*A History of the University of Natal* (Pietermaritzburg, 1966), 45.

15　Champion papers, University of South Africa, 2 [3.1.8] Mabel Palmer to Champion, 13 Feb. 1930.

16　Ibid.

17　Ibid. [3.1.9.] Champion to Mabel Palmer, 17 Feb. 1930.

18　According to an interview with Lily and her sister, Alpheus Ndhlovu, then a law student at Cape Town, suggested she write to Mabel Palmer. On being contacted in 1985, Ndhlovu vaguely recalled his pen-friendship, but had no recollection of Mabel Palmer.

19　Lily Moya (henceforth LM) to Mabel Palmer (henceforth MP), 4 Jan 1949. Here and elsewhere in the text I have retained the original spelling, punctuation and usage in the correspondence. I have inserted corrections or explanations in the notes only where there is a danger of non-comprehension or confusion. The introduction of the scholarly convention [sic] where the misspelling is in the original would have been intrusive in these letters.

20　MP to NC, 14 April 1949. Native Commissioners in South Africa had extensive administrative and judicial powers over Africans in the 'reserves' similar to those exerted by their counterparts in colonial Africa.

21　Frank Molteno, 'The historical foundations of schooling of black South Africans', in P. Kallaway, ed. *Apartheid and Education: the education of black South Africans* (Johannesburg, 1984), 91—3.

22　UG 53—1951 *Report on Native Education in South Africa,* paras. 689—93.

23　M. Horrell, *Bantu Education to 1968* (SAIRR, Johannesburg, 1968), 1.

24　Cited in Molteno, 'Historical foundations', 66.

25　LM to MP, 30 Aug. 1949.

26　For a fascinating account of the nature of education in colonial Africa, and especially the notion of 'the school in the bush', see A. Victor Murray's book of that title, published in London in 1929.

27　Nongqause was a Xhosa prophetess who, in 1856 at a time of great national distress as a result of colonial conquest and disruption as well as drought, maintained that if the Xhosa killed all their cattle, destroyed their crops and smashed all tools of European provenance, their ancestors would return, and restore their ancient prosperity and power. The result of the cattle-killing was mass starvation and thousands of destitute Xhosa streamed across the Kei river to seek work amongst the colonists. The discrediting of the prophecy and the dislocation in social life also led vast numbers of Xhosa to turn to Christianity for the first time. The cattle-killing thus became a key event in the mission history of the region: for many the starting point of 'civilisation'.

28 LM to MP, 1 Feb. 1950.
29 LM to MP, 12 Oct. 1949.
30 MP to LM, 4 Jan. 1950.
31 Ibid.
32 The early days of St Cuthbert's Mission are described in A.G.S. Gibson, *Eight Years in Kaffraria* (London, 1893); this section is also based on St Augustine's *Occasional Papers*, no.2, 1884, and *Occasional News from St Cuthbert's*, no.1, 1900, 'Bransby Lewis Key, Bishop'. That the attack began on the Mfengu was hardly surprising. As Key described it:

> Colonies of half-civilised families, mostly Christian, pushing, industrious, and I may say grasping, came to settle among the raw Pondomisi — came with their new-fangled ways, used to colonial law and order, ready to cringe to the chief to get his lands, but secretly despising him. . . . The history of the next seven years would be almost filled with the account of the squabbles which ensued between the Fingoes and the Pondomisi.

33 Molteno, 'Historical foundations', 57.
34 The names are of course fictional, but what follows is based upon documentary sources as well as oral evidence. Alice's father is mentioned in St Augustine's *Occasional Papers*, no.2, 1884 as a schoolteacher; she is first mentioned as having been confirmed at the Girls' Industrial school at the end of 1896 (St Cuthbert's *Mission Report*, 1896). The church reports are to be found in the Church of the Province Archives, University of Witwatersrand. This section and much of what follows is based both on these mission records and on oral information from Lily's sister and mother, and is borne out by documentary sources, both in the Anglican Archives at the University of Witwatersrand and in the Cape Archives. Above all, I am grateful to Ms Manthe B. Nkotsoe of African Studies Institute, University of Witwatersrand, for two tapes of interviews with the Moya family, made in November 1982, and to Denis Mashabela in July, 1984. I was able to interview them myself in July 1983, thanks to the assistance of Professor Charles van Onselen and his oral historians at the ASI, especially Moses Molepo.

35 St Augustine's, *Occasional Paper*, 1890 and St Cuthbert's *Mission Report*, 1895, 17, 21.

36 Before that he was assisted by one of his sisters. In 1901, Alice is listed as Assistant Teacher and Sewing Mistress (St Cuthbert's *Mission Report*, 1898–1901).

37 G. Callaway, to his mother, 14 June 1899, p.147, in E.D. Sedding (ed.) 'Letters of Godfrey Callaway, Missionary in Kaffraria, 1892–1942', n.d. TSS, from St Cuthbert's library, Tsolo, now in the Church of the Province Archives, University of Witwatersrand.

38 For his success as a teacher, see *Mission Reports*, 1898–1900.

39 Molteno, 'Historical foundations', 53.

40 For an important account of the role of headmen in the Ciskei as allies of the colonial state and the possibilities of accumulation which their position opened up, see J. Lewis, 'An economic history of the Ciskei, 1848–1900', Ph.D., University of Cape Town, 1984, vol.2, pp. 593ff. Although Lewis deals with the Ciskei before 1900, it is likely that his remarks apply to the more easterly Transkeian territories somewhat later. For the significance of the personal example of the new elite in helping 'to change [African] social structure to fit in with European concepts of work and interpersonal relationships', and their wider role as intermediaries, see also P. Kallaway, 'Introduction' in P. Kallaway, ed. *Apartheid and Education*, 9.

41 Cape Archives, CMT 3/925 File copy 7782/6724, Dec. 1916. I have to thank Dr William Beinart for leading me to the relevant file and Dr Christopher Saunders for finding the letter for me.

42 See W. Beinart and C. Bundy, 'State intervention and rural resistance: the Transkei, 1900–1965', in M. Klein (ed.), *Peasants in Africa* (Beverley Hills, 1980), 285.

43 Ibid. 287–8.

44 Ibid.

45 Oral information from Moya family, July 1983. It is not entirely clear whether Daniel and Henry held their lands on individual tenure, or whether the property was held communally; I have been unable to track down their wills in the Cape Archives, which suggests that the local oral tradition that these were communal lands is correct. The land was, nonetheless, handed down to the eldest son by primogeniture on their deaths. I am grateful to Ms Rosalie Kingwill for field research in the Transkei which has substantiated much of the above.

46 Oral interview, November, 1982. For the East and some West African examples, see N. Nelson, unpublished paper presented to the conference on the history of the family in Africa, SOAS, September 1981.

47   LM to MP, 20 May 1949.

48   LM to MP, 14 June 1949.

49   MP to LM, 17 June 1949.

50   Black Christians in South Africa of Lily's background would have shared the vision of C.L.R. James, expressed in a recent interview in *Third World Book Review* (vol.1, no.2, 1984, p.7):

> *Review*: Some Caribbean intellectuals of your generation could be accused of excessive veneration for Western culture and of implicitly downgrading the African and New World roots of their own languages and culture.
>
> James: I do not know what are the African roots of the language and culture of Caribbean intellectuals. . . . The basis of our civilisation in the Caribbean is an adaptation of Western civilisation.
>
> *Review*: But *should* Shakespeare and Rembrandt and Beethoven matter to Caribbean people?
>
> James: The Caribbean people are *people*, and Shakespeare, Rembrandt and Beethoven should matter to *all* people who are living in the world today, and who are able by means of their language or by their means of information and communication to understand or get some insight into what Shakespeare and Beethoven mean. I don't like that question at all.

The Eastern Cape is, of course not the Caribbean, and Xhosa culture and language were and are deeply part of Christian Xhosa culture; but the acceptance of a common heritage drawn from the classics of European culture would, before the advent of Bantu education at least, have been shared.

51   See especially MP to G. C. Grant, 26 May 1950 and MP to LM, 4 Jan. 1950.

52   Vietzen, 'Fabian transplant', 9.

53   G. C. Grant, *Adams College 1853–1951* (Printed by the *Natal Witness*, n.d. c.1951), 1.

54   Luthuli briefly describes his teaching at Adams in his autobiography, *Let my people go* (London, 1862), 34–42; Z. K. Matthews talks of his experiences (even more briefly) in *Freedom For My People: the autobiography of Z. K. Matthews: Southern Africa 1901–1968* (Cape Town and Johannesburg, 1981), 85–92.

55   Grant, *Adams College*, 1–3.

56   Ibid, 5.

57   Of these professions, only medicine demanded a matriculation entrance qualification for training.

58   Grant, *Adams College*, 5.

59   LM to MP, 12 Sept 1950, below.

60   For an elaboration of this position, see J. J. Guy, 'Analysing pre-

capitalist societies in southern Africa'. Unpublished paper presented to the seminar on the 'Societies of Southern Africa in the 19th and 20th centuries', Institute of Commonwealth Studies, London, May, 1986.

61 Revd J. L. Dube, 'The arrest of progress of Christianity among the heathen tribes of South Africa', in *The Evangelisation of South Africa. Report of the Sixth General Missionary Conference of South Africa, held at Johannesburg, June 30th – July 3rd 1925* (Cape Town, 1925), 64.

62 The quotation is from R. Q. Gray, *The Labour Aristocracy in Victorian Edinburgh* (Oxford, 1976) 142, cited in J. Weeks, *Sex, Politics and Society: the regulation of sexuality since 1800* (London and New York, 1981) 74, on which this draws heavily.

63 Society for the Propagation of the Gospel Archives, London, vol.D.65, 1883: Report of Revd Bishop Bransby Key for the year ending Dec. 31st 1883. I am grateful to Lara Marks for finding this for me.

64 *Occasional News of St Cuthbert's*, 1905, 7. Letter from Fr. Puller, 3 Nov. 1905.

65 For the 'alarm' over 'purity' amongst African women, see D. Gaitskell's illuminating essay, 'Wailing for purity: prayer unions, African mothers and adolescent daughters, 1912–1940' in S. Marks and R. Rathbone, *Industrialisation and Social Change: African class formation, culture and consciousness, 1870–1930* (London, 1982). The problem was not unique to South Africa, or to Christian women, however. In contemporary Zambia, for example, Bonnie B. Keller writes:

> Girls, from the age of thirteen to fourteen, are under pressure to begin sexual relationships. Typically pressure comes from older men – who are themselves married. One inevitable result of the emphasis on early female sexuality is a high rate of pregnancy among girls in grades six and seven and among grade seven school leavers ... ('Marriage and medicine: women's search for love and luck', *African Social Research*, 26 December 1978, pp. 489–505. Quotation from 493).

The administrative concern is expressed in the letters between MP and the Native Commissioner, Umtata, 14 April 1949. For the Bantu Youth League, see above, p.34.

66 For the strains on women imposed by the migrant labour system, see, for example, L. Clarke and J. Ngobese, *Women without Men* (Durban, 1975).

67 It is difficult to know how much of this was directed personally at Lily. In the 1920s, Gilbert Coka recalled his experience of initiation at Adams:

Hardly had he [the Principal] departed than the teachers also vanished. Belts were out in moment and the older students were giving us a flogging. We were newcomers and didn't know whither to escape. After a while, the teachers entered and the belts disappeared. On our way upstairs the tale was repeated. We crouched into our beds like malefactors. Hardly had the lights been blown when we heard footfalls. Blows showered upon us. We were afraid to scream. The older students with whom we shared the dormitory condoled with us and said that it was college custom . . . (in M. Perham, ed. *Ten Africans*, (London, 1936) 291).

68 The phrase is an interesting one in view of the title of I.B. Thabata's later work on Bantu education, *Education for Barbarism*, published in 1959. An Eastern Cape intellectual, Thabata was at the time President of the Trotskyite Non-European Unity Movement. Lily's use of the phrase suggests it was in common currency in the 1940s and 1950s.

69 LM to MP, 3 June 1951.

70 American Board Archives, Harvard (henceforth AB) 15.4, vol.4:17, Lavinia Scott (Principal, Inanda) to R. Emerson (Secretary, ABM, Boston) 27 Nov. 1940; and ibid. 14 Nov. 1941.

71 Killie Campbell Africana Library, (henceforth KCAL) MS ADA 1.07 Adams High School Reports, Minutes of General Purposes Committee, Adams, 10 May 1946, p.4. The seduction of African schoolgirls by their schoolmasters was common gossip in South African high schools in the 1940s and 1950s. It was said that teachers would frequently bribe male students to 'confess', if the girl fell pregnant, in order to keep their positions (personal communication, Professor John Blacking, Belfast, May 1985). See also the title story in Njabula Ndebele's *Fools and Other Stories* (Johannesburg, 1984). The problem is by no means over. According to *Africa Business*, no 63, 'Zimbabwe's government is sacking and jailing amorous male teachers who have been responsible for impregnating their pupils. So far 25 out of the 500 teachers in the Gurube district have been fired. . . . Declared the Minister of Education: "Our schools are not maternity wards." ' Cited in *New Internationalist*, no. 132, February, 1984.

72 MP to Sister Edista, 15 June 1951; there were about 275 boys to 175 girls at Adams in 1949.

73 A. Vilakazi, *Zulu Transformations* (Pietermaritzburg, 1965), 102.

74 R. Hunt Davis, Jun., 'Charles T. Loram and the American model for South African education in South Africa', in P. Kallaway (ed.) *Education and Apartheid*, 108–126. This was originally published in *African Studies Review*, XIX, 2, 1976. As Hunt Davis summarises Loram's views, Africans suffered from genuine social and economic

disabilities, 'but they were as yet immature in their stage of civilisation ... as yet they remained a subject race in need of betterment. Therefore, whites had to decide what was best for Africans. . . .' The education of Africans was for Loram not an end in itself, but a means of maintaining a segregated society. A lack of schools would create discontent among Africans and threaten the status quo, but so would an education that raised African expectations beyond a certain level. Schools, then, were one of the key weapons in the 'battle of race adjustment' that was taking place. For Loram's biography, see Hunt Davis, op.cit., and a valuable unpublished MSS by Martin Legassick, 'C.T. Loram and South African "Native policy", 1920–1929'. According to Lavinia Scott, Loram 'was one of the greatest friends the African people have had, either here or in the US ...' (AB 15.4 vol. 4:17, Lavinia Scott to Mabel Emerson, 23 July 1940). African leaders were rather less sure. A. W. G. Champion, the ICU leader was scathing in his criticism: for example, see Champion to *Ilanga lase Natal* 1 Feb. 1930.

75 Hunt Davis, 'Charles T. Loram and the American model', 113–6.

76 See LM to MP, 17 May 1951.

77 N.C. Manganyi, *Looking Through the Keyhole: dissenting essays on the black experience* (Johannesburg, 1981), 16–17.

78 *Down Second Avenue* (London, 1959) 145.

79 In 1929 Thomas Jesse Jones of the Phelps-Stokes Fund described Adams as 'among the most notable schools in Africa' (*The Missionary Herald*, June 1929).

80 KCAL, Webb Papers, KCM 22098, Brookes to M. Webb, July 1947.

81 For the troubled history of Adams in the 1940s, see KCAL, KCAV Interview with E. Brookes, op.cit. and AB 15.4 vol.51 and 53 *passim*. For the upheavals in August, 1950, Grant to Parents and Governors, 18 Aug. 1950; Minutes of a Special Meeting of the General Purposes Committee, Adams, 7th Sept. 1949 (KCAL MS ADA 1.07, Adams College Minutes) and Mrs Ida Grant's letter to friends, 8 Oct. 1950, where she describes the episode as 'an unhappy setback' and 'a heavy disappointment', I am grateful to Mrs Grant for showing me this correspondence. For the expulsion of the two students in June 1949 see Adams High School Reports, Minutes of General Purposes Committee, Report no.2, 24 June 1949 (KCAL, MS ADA 1.07).

82 For the atmosphere more generally in the African high schools and colleges, see B. Hirson, *Year of Ash, Year of Fire. The Soweto revolt: roots of a revolution?* (London, 1979), 30–6 and F. Molteno, 'Historical foundations', 74–99 and 94 ff; Hirson does not mention the Adams disturbances specifically and Molteno only alludes to them briefly. For the salience of ethnic identity in Natal in the 1940s, see S. Marks, 'Patriotism, patriarchy and purity: Natal and

the politics of Zulu ethnic consciousness', in Leroy Vail, *The Political Economy of Ethnicity in Southern Africa* (forthcoming).

83 LM to MP, 2 Jan. 1951.

84 MP to LM, 12 Jan. 1951.

85 See LM to MP, 16 Jan. 1951; Reports, 4 Dec. 1950 and June, 1951; LM to MP 24 Jan. 1951, 28 Jan. 1951, 8 Feb. 1951, 4 April, 1951.

86 Lily clearly disliked the new Dean and describes her as 'ruling with an iron hand', to MP, 17 May 1951.

87 Sibusisiwe Makhanya (henceforth SM) to MP, 14 Aug. 1951.

88 The phrase is from Myrtle Trowbridge's unpublished biography of Sibusisiwe Makhanya, simply entitled 'Sibusisiwe' (which means 'We are blessed') (n.d., KCAL, 3 parts, KCM 14343–5), p.4. I have drawn heavily on this text in what follows.

89 The phrases are, in order of quotation, from KCM 14344, Trowbridge, 'Sibusisiwe', Part 2, p.62; AB 15.4 vol.41, p.656, M. Walbridge to M. Emerson, 20 June 1927; and 'Miss Makhanya in Boston', *The Missionary Herald*, November 1927, p.411.

90 See above,

91 For Loram, see Note 74 above.

92 The Jeanes teachers were so-called after the American philanthropist, Anna T. Jeanes, a Philadelphian Quaker, who left a bequest of £200,000 to improve small country schools for children in the southern United States. The emphasis of Jeanes teaching was on fitting the students for life, with hygiene, gardening, needlework and community work given a high priority. Loram described the work at Penn School as 'the finest experiment in linking home and school and in curriculum making that some of us have seen in any school, white, black or yellow, in any part of the world', Moton Papers, Tuskegee, General Correspondence, Box 187, 1589, TSS, 'The Negro college at the crossroads', n.d. c.1933–4. For Jeanes teaching and its application in Africa, see K.J. King, *Pan-Africanism and Education: a study of race philanthropy and education in the southern states and of America and East Africa* (London, 1971), and R. Hunt Davis, 'Producing the "Good African": South Carolina's Penn School as a Guide for African Education in South Africa', in A.T. Mogomba and N. Nyaggah, *Independence without Freedom: the political economy of colonial education in southern Africa* (Santa Barbara, 1980), 83–112, and 'Charles T. Loram', p.93–6. For a contemporary critique of the application of the Phelps-Stokes/Jesse Jones philosophy to Africa, see A. Victor Murray, *The School in the Bush*, esp. pp.305–10.

93 For Sibusisiwe's sojourn in the United States and break with Loram and Phelps-Stokes, see R. Hunt Davis, Jun., 'Producing the "Good African" ', op.cit. For the detailed reasons for her break with Phelps-

Stokes, see her long itemised letter to C.T. Loram from Cleveland, 30 Sept. 1928, a copy of which was found in the Moton Papers, Tuskegee, General Correspondence, Box 141 (1104). See also AB 15.4. vol 48 *passim*. For the evidence that she was not alone in her discontent, see K. J. King, *Pan-Africanism and Education*, 225–31. Among South Africans, apparently the composer, R. T. Caluza shared her views: John Dube cast them together in a letter to T. J. Jones as 'very ambitious and often unreasonable and ungrateful'. See Phelps-Stokes Fund Papers, Schomburg Library, New York, RG General Administrative Records, TJJ to C. T. Loram, 3 May 1931.

94 Mabel Carney was very much part of the 'race relations' network which Sibusisiwe was trying to escape, though she seems to have been rather more sympathetic and sensitive in her approach. Born in 1885 and brought up in Oklahoma, she became interested in rural education as a result of her own educational experiences. She first entered the Columbia Teachers College, New York, as a student in 1909 and re-entered for graduate study in 1917, producing her *Country Life and the Country School* which the *Cape Argus* (31 May 1926) enthusiastically described at the time of her visit to South Africa as 'one of the earliest and one of the standard works on the subject'. Before taking her position at the Teachers College, she acted as state inspector for rural schools for many years. She retired from Columbia in 1942 to Marseilles, Illinois, where she died. See Columbia Teachers College, President's Files, 184 and 187: Mabel Carney, and Second Dean Russell's files. Mabel Carney also influenced the thinking of Loram and South Africa's best known educationalist, E.G. Malherbe, both of whom studied at the TC. (See Malherbe's autobiography, *Never a Dull Moment* [Cape Town, 1981]). The quotation is from Dean W.F. Russell to M.C. Langford, 6 March 1945, Second Dean Russell's Files, TC.

95 Trowbridge, 'Sibusisiwe', Part II, pp.109–110.

96 Ibid. p. 114.

97 Ibid.

98 D.H. Reader, *Zulu Tribe in Transition: the Makhanya of Southern Natal* (Manchester, 1966), 342. One cannot help feeling that Reader's conclusions were shaped by the way in which Sibusisiwe herself had adapted western and Zulu norms.

99 I use the term 'traditional' with reluctance. By the 1950s, the Makhanya people had been influenced by colonial mores for over a century.

100 Reader, *Zulu Tribe in Transition*, 113.

101 Trowbridge, 'Sibusisiwe', 113.

102 AB 15.4 vol.50, Lavinia Scott, Adams, 7 June 1933 to 'Dear Friends'. Cyclostyled letter.

103 Loram papers, Yale University, Box 1, File 46. National Education. n.d. *c.* 1927.

104 *Rural Education Newsletter*, no.1, 1 Jan. 1935. (Found at Columbia Teachers College). In 1933 Mabel Carney called Sibusisiwe 'the most outstanding native African woman in the world today' (Trowbridge, 'Sibusisiwe', 114).

105 AB 15.4 vol.50. Lavinia Scott, Adams, 7 June 1933, to 'Dear Friends'. Cyclostyled letter.

106 A. P. Stokes papers, Yale University, Box 175, Folder 8, Series III. Recommendations and commitments made by Dr Stokes during his African tour, 1932–3.

107 Lionel Forman Papers, University of Cape Town, BC 581 A1.35. A. W. G. Champion to S. Makhanya, 20 Nov. 1929.

108 Moton Papers, Tuskegee, Box 150 (1189). S. Makhanya to R. Moton, 30 April 1930.

109 For the change from a pan-South African to a Zulu ethnic nationalism among Natal's intelligentsia at this time, see S. Marks, *The Ambiguities of Dependence*, chapter 2. In the 1930s Sibusisiwe was an adviser to the Zulu Society, in whose Charter there were explicit references to the breakdown of 'traditional' discipline, particularly in relation to women and youth. Cf. Appendix to the Charter of the Zulu Society, 1939:

> Par. 24. It is alarming since it [i.e. the 'departure from wholesome Zulu traditions'] is undermining the calm dignity of our women. We are perplexed, and we involuntarily ask: If our women lose the dignity and favour which are their natural possessions, then who will mother the future men of rank and the leaders and counsellors who will sustain the Zulus as a people for ever? . . . 40. There is a danger of a general collapse of the *Ukuhlonipa* etiquette of women and girls, which is leaning away from custom. Owing to a falling away from custom, women and girls are losing their wholesome respect which was to their credit and which their presence inspired in family life. This causes a slackening of the solidarity and sacredness of the whole Home Life of a man, which was to be found there before, and in this manner, Home Life is being desecrated and disintegrated and good customs abandoned. (Natal Archives Acc. no 302. The Charter of the Zulu Society.)

For an analysis of the Zulu Society and Zulu ethnic politics, see my 'Patriotism, patriarchy and purity: Natal and the politics of cultural nationalism'.

110 KCAL, KCAV 139 Interview between A. Manson and H. M. S. Makhanya, 13 June 1979.

111　KCAL, KCAV 110 Interview between A. Manson and E. Brookes, 14 Feb. 1979.

112　AB 15.4 vol.3:10 Edgar Brookes to J. Reuling, 1 Aug. 1947.

113　Trowbridge, 'Sibusisiwe', p.122.

114　See above, p.31.

115　AB 15.4 vol.55, 5:19. Report on Mbumbulu, received 7 May 1947.

116　Trowbridge, 'Sibusisiwe', p.81.

117　KCAL, KCAV 139 Interview with H. M. S. Makhanya, 19 March 1979. There are also hints of resentment at her sexual independence in the unpublished TSS of her life by M. Trowbridge in the Killie Campbell Africana Library, KCM 14345. See especially p.130.

118　LM to MP, 4 April 1951.

119　MP to SM, 20 Jan. 1951; MP to SM, 4 Nov. 1950; LM to MP, 4 April 1951.

120　MP to SM, 6 June 1951.

121　SM to MP, 8 June 1951.

122　MP to Sister Edista, Mariannhill, 15 June 1951.

123　Vilakazi, *Zulu Transformations*, 94–106. Quotation is on 100.

124　MP to LM,, 7 June 1951.

125　Vietzen ('Fabian transplant', 7) describes Mabel Palmer as

>　a comical figure in her latter years. To protect her poor eyesight and tremendously thick spectacles, she unashamedly wore a tennis-peak-like green eyeshade wherever she went. She would sit in meetings, Senate no less, complete with eyeshade, and knit, and when boredom overcame her completely, she would turn out her specially made monstrous leather handbag and noisily count her change. Added to this were the various implications of her great rotundity. Thus, a combination of poor eyesight and large girth — which prevented her from bending — meant that she devised the ingenious scheme of doing her gardening on her tummy . . .

>　Under the circumstances, it is perhaps not surprising that she grew somewhat acerbic with the unfortunate Lily.

126　Record of telephone conversation with Mr Havermann, 16 July 1951.

127　LM to MP, 26 July 1951.

128　SM to MP, 31 July 1951.

The Correspondence

Box 30, Umtata
4th Jan. 1949

The Organizer for,
The Non-European Section,
The University of Natal,
Durban.

Dear Madam,

I can be very pleased if you can take me in your college as a boarding student. I do n't moralise when I tell you that I'm a helpless orphan. I have obtained this educational status through my being a day-scholar student, due only to my financial embarrasment.[1]

I believe being a boarding student in college is more encouraging and beneficial to a student in studies and all. It does n't matter whether you take me in this year to complete the Matriculation Course.[2] That is much better than staying at home so young as I am.

If you can answer me at your earliest possible I can be very glad. Think of it – competing with much previleged students, boarders, a day-scholar in Matric.

I beg for your sincere sympathy,

I am,
Yours truly,
Lily P. Moya

1. In fact, the school, St John's College, Umtata, did not take girl students as boarders.
2. Matriculation was the final school-leaving examination.

The Registrar,
Natal University,
Warwick Avenue,
Durban.

Dear Sir,

I hereby beg you to grant me with a bursary scholarship to educate me from this year onwards until I finish my degree course.

In 1948 I had been a candidate for the Senior Certificate Examination.[1] All along I had been learning as a day scholar student up to the matriculation Course II. I had to compete with students who are Boarders in Colleges, and I had to undergo some difficulties, but I have tried my level best to get better class positions.

Relatives have been tried to help me in education but in vain. I have tried all means to apply for nursing but has been refused because I haven't reached the required age and due to my smallness.

I was borne in 1933, August, 31st. I am a poor and helpless orphan. I do n't think there can be anyone who can impede me from coming to your university should you be sympathetic to me.

I had a mind of carrying my education privately through the Correspondence College, but I have been informed that the student has to pay some tuition. There is no one who can pay for me, I am an orphan.

I should be very glad if you would answer to my humble request at your earliest possible.

I am,
Yours truly,
Lily P. Moya

1. The Cape Senior Certificate examination was the equivalent of the matriculation examination elsewhere in the Union. For the numbers of Africans reaching matriculation, see Introduction, p.9.

Natal University College, Durban
15th January, 1949

Miss Lily P. Moya,
Box 30,
Umtata.

Dear Miss Moya,

I have read your letter with considerable sympathy but I do not know that there is much that I can do for you. Students are only admitted to this College [1] if they have already passed the Matriculation examination or its equivalent, and we could not possibly admit you until you have completed your Cape Senior Certificate, and completed it in such a way that it is recognized as equivalent to matriculation. Nor would you be eligible for any of our bursaries until that time.

I do not want to discourage you, but it is obvious also from your letter that you have not yet sufficient command of English to make it likely that you could appreciate University lectures delivered in English.

You do not tell me what is your occupation, but I feel that the best thing that you can do is to continue to work either for the Cape Senior or preferably for the matriculation examination, or perhaps in some ways this is the best suggestion, for the Senior Commercial Examination (Matriculation Equivalent). The advantage of the latter is that part-time students are allowed to take it in two parts, whereas they must pass the whole matriculation examination at one sitting.

Could you give me the names of one or two people who know you in Umtata so that we can consider whether there is anyway in which we might get a little help for you?

Much the best thing would be for you to be entered as a student at Adams College,[2] to complete your matriculation as a student there and subsequently come on to us.

If you would write me a further account of yourself with reference to one or two people who know you, so that I could consider whether there is any direction in which we could help

1. Natal University College; from 15 March 1949 the University of Natal.
2. For Adams, see Introduction, pp.19—20.

you, but it would not be help given by the University of Natal which is given completely to post matriculation work.

I am not sending any forms as I am quite certain you are not eligible to enter, but I will send you a prospectus as soon as possible which will show you the kind of work we do here.

Yours sincerely,

Dr Mabel Palmer

Box 30, Umtata
26th Jan. 1949

The Organizer of The Non-European Section,
Natal University College, Durban.

Madam,

Many thanks for the reply you gave to my previous letter. I am an orphan with no property, a student, borne on the 31st August 1933. All along I had been learning as a day scholar student, due to financial embarrasment. Even clothing and the paying of my school fees for day-schooling has been a great burden for me.

In 1948 I had been a candidate for the Senior Certificate (Matriculation Course II). The results have n't come yet but I have heard rumours that I have n't gone through. Perhaps it may be due to the fact that I had n't sufficient time for doing my work. I had to labour very hard after school and sometimes had to go to school without meals.

Mine is a very sad case. I can be very thankful to you if you can take me into college this year to complete this Matriculation Course, if I have really failed, or to go to the University.

I had no chance at all to do my school work − homework, and I believe that boarders have sufficient time to do their work.

Should I be taken in a school near to a University I can be more pleased. I'm really sad about this matter − financial embarrassed, there is no-one who can help me. I like education.

Kindly sympathise with me, a helpless orphan,[1] I beg you. The great number of people know me. Elderly men like Mr Wm

1. See Introduction, p.17.

58

Piliso, R.M.O., Umtata,[2] and Mr C. Bam, the Grassland Farms,[3] Tsolo, and others and some women.

I can be very glad if you answer me at your earliest possible and please I beg you do sympathise with. You can only show your sympathy by taking me to a college where I shall work with my level best my school work, and, I'm sure I'll please you in any way in my character.

I am,

Yours truly

Lily P. Moya

Box 30, Umtata
7/2/49

The Organiser of The Non-European Section,
Natal University College, Durban.

Madam,

Don't be surprised to receive a letter after another. I wish you can be ensured that I really don't moralise when I tell you that I have no means at all of carrying on my education without monetary assistance.

I'm an orphan. I'm not in school now because there is no-one who can pay for my fees nor for the boarding and lodging at any place here at Umtata so that I may carry on as a day scholar.

Kindly consider this and be sympathetic to me. There is only one way you can show your sympathy – by taking me in your school to complete my Matric. Course. This is the only way significant to show you how I'm really worried.

I can be very glad if you can answer me at your earliest possible – and please be sympathetic.

I am,

Yours truly,

Lily P. Moya

2. William Piliso had his B.Sc. and worked as a Hygiene teacher at St John's, Umtata. R.M.O. stands for Resident Magistrate's Office.
3. The Bam family were prominent in Transkei affairs. C. Bam was apparently working at this time in the office of the Transkei Regional Council, or Bunga, in Umtata.

The Organizer, Non-European Section,
Natal University College, Durban.

Dear Madam,

Still I'm anxiously waiting for yours in reply to the successive requests I made to you. I'm still at home not in school, only due to financial embarrassment. My heart aches when I see other children having gone and still going to school.

I humbly beg you to sympathise with me. The only way you can show your sympathies is by taking me in your College to complete this Matriculation Course this year.

Really there is no other way possible for me to carry on my education without your monetary assistance. Do n't put me in for the coming year — would die if I stay a whole year out of school.

Other students are going ahead with their studies while I'm still at home. Can be very glad if you answer me Miss, — and call for me into your school before the end of this month or at least at the beginning of March.

How can I show you that I really mean what I say to you and that it is truth? I hope you'll answer me, will always be in watch of a letter from you and hope for your kindness to and sympathy with me.

With best wishes,

I am,
Yours sincerely,
Lily P. Moya

Natal University College, Durban
28 February, 1949

Miss Lily P. Moya,
Box 30, Umtata.

Dear Miss Moya,

I am sorry I have kept you waiting, but unfortunately I cannot admit you to this College. It is only for post matriculants, but your last letter interested me so much and I am so anxious to do something for you, that I suggest the following plan.

The M.L. Sultan Technical College in Durban[1] would be prepared to admit you as a student for matriculation. The fees will be £8/10/- and might be reduced on recommendation from someone whom the College authorities know and trust.

I suggest that your best plan is to come to Durban and to try and get work. Are you good with children? Could you possibly undertake work as a nursemaid on the understanding that you are to be free to attend these part time classes?

It is quite impossible for me to find any funds to support you in Durban. You would have to find some work for that, and unless you got a suitable living in position you would have to stay at the women's hostel which is not a very agreeable place.[2]

I would be prepared to advance your railway fare if you would send me a note of this, and I would also ask you to be willing to be placed under the supervision of an older Zulu woman, as I think you are a bit too young to be quite on your own in a big town like Durban. I have a very suitable person who helps in our library who I think would undertake that.

I am sorry that I have nothing else to suggest, but I think that very probably this would work. There is a very considerable demand in Durban for responsible and educated girls in domestic service.[3] I cannot think of any other branch of work in which you would be likely to find a place. I think you would have to be prepared to work as a domestic servant, but if you

1. The M.L. Sultan Technical College was founded in 1946 as a result of a generous financial contribution made by M.L. Sultan, a leading Indian merchant in Durban, in 1946. Initially open to African as well as Indian children, it was forced to restrict its intake to Indians only after 1956 (under the Vocational Educational Act of 1955), as a condition for further government support.
2. The Durban African Women's Hostel was founded as a result of missionary pressure by the Durban Corporation in the second decade of the century. For its reputation see MP to LM, 14.4.49, and MP to NC, Umtata, 14.4.49.
3. Mabel's suggestion that Lily become a domestic servant could not have been very welcome: it was precisely her role as domestic servant in Umtata which she was trying to escape through becoming a boarder. The correspondence sheds a great deal of light on the openings available for African women in South Africa in the middle of the century: see below, e.g. MP to LM, 12.1.51 and 21.6.51.

61

are as keen on education as you say you are, I think you will be willing to do that.

You must of course be sure that all your necessary passes are in order.

If you would let me know when you are arriving in Durban I will ask the Zulu lady under whose supervision I am thinking of putting you, if she would be willing to meet you and to help you to find your way about Durban.

Yours sincerely,
Mabel Palmer

P.O. Box 30, Umtata
4.3.49

My dear Miss Palmer,

Many thanks for yours, I have recently received. Any advice leading to education is very essential to me. You have really consoled me. I do n't know how to thank you to equal to what you have done for me.

I'm well prepared to come to Durban. As soon as you have payed for my train fare and informed me of it I shall come. I am very anxious to be in school.

My nearest railway station is at Umtata. Will you tell me yours. On Monday or on the day of my leave I'll ask for the pass.

Can't you give me the date I should entrain for Durban because I'm not a great traveller. I mean to say I'm not sure of how many days I would take to reach Durban and of the Station I shall come to.

With greetings and love,

Yours sincerely,
Lily P. Moya

Miss L.P. Moya,
P.O. Box 30, Umtata.

Dear Miss Moya,

I must admit I was rather taken aback by your letter of the 4th March. If you are not, yourself, capable of making arrangements for your railway journey from Umtata, how are you going to be able to look after yourself in Durban even with the assistance of Miss Thabethe, who is the Bantu lady under whose supervision I wish you to place yourself.

She tells me that it would be very unwise of you to come to Durban until you have secured accommodation at the hostel, and that you should write to the

> Matron,
> Women's Hostel,
> Grey Street, Durban

explaining your circumstances and asking them if you can be accepted.

You must clearly understand that I cannot in any way support you in Durban. You must do that yourself.

If you can manage to come to Durban, get a place to live in and get work so that you can support yourself, I shall be pleased to take you to the office of the M.L. Sultan Technical College and arrange for your enrolment in their matriculation classes, but you would of course, have to find work that would enable you to attend these classes.

If you could write to me and tell me what is the railway fare from Umtata and by what train you propose to travel, and what time it arrives in Durban so that Miss Thabethe can meet you, and can assure me that you have secured accommodation at the Women's Hostel, then I will send you your railway fare and help you in enrolling in the Technical College, but please understand that I will not give anything towards your support in Durban. I am not a rich woman and I could not undertake any such responsibility, but if you can get over these various difficulties *yourself* then I will be pleased to give you any help I can in the way of advice and assistance other than monetary assistance.

I am sorry to seem a little abrupt. I am very anxious to help a girl who is as anxious for education as you seem to be, but if that girl is so impracticable that she cannot even arrange her own railway journey and let me know the cost of it, I must say that I am beginning to be a little doubtful whether it is wise to tell that girl to come to Durban.

However, I hope you will surmount these difficulties and that I shall see you before long.

Yours sincerely,
Mabel Palmer

Also you should have the consent of your guardian otherwise I might get into trouble with the authorities.

Corporation of the City of Durban
Native Women's Hostel, Grey Street
29th March 1949

Miss Lily P. Moya,
P.O. Box 30, Umtata.

Dear Miss Moya,

Your letter of the 22nd., inst. to hand and in reply I have to tell you that we have no accommodation and further more that we cannot in any case take students, as this is a hostel for working girls. I would advise you to contact the magistrate of your District, without whose permission you may not leave Umtata, he may be helpful in placing you elsewhere.

Yours faithfully,
N. Gutridge
Rel. Matron

Box 30, Umtata
30.3.49

The Organizer, Non-European Section,
Natal University College, Durban.

Dear Madam,

Many thanks for yours although it is a little bit now doubtful. Anyway I trust that He[1] will make this successful. I do understand that you may be having some trouble in trying to help some-one you have never seen before, but, I still beg you, do not withdraw. My only wish is just obtaining this education and to finish this Course this year.

The train-fare from Kokstad to Durban is £1.10.8 (One pound ten shillings and eightpence) and the bus fare from Umtata to Kokstad is 15/- in the Express bus. That means to say that the whole journey fare is £2. 5/8. Be sure that if there is even a penny surplus to the journey fare you have sent to me I shall tell you the truth and shall give it back to you. I shall take the Kokstad line, because I have been advised that it is a less expensive line.[2]

I have written to the matron[3] as your advise. I posted that letter on the 24th instant. There is no reply yet. Do not delay, you see dear Miss send it to me. Other children are going a-head with their studies.

I can be very glad if you can take me affectionately and let no other person nor thing restrict you from helping me,

I'm still in great grief and hope for your earliest reply. With greetings and love,

> I am,
> Yours sincerely,
> Lily P. Moya

P.S. I hope to see you very soon. Be sure I won't bring you any trouble — I have the full consent of my guardian of coming there.
'The Same'

---

1. i.e. God. This is the first indication in the correspondence of Lily's intense religious feeling.
2. Lily had an aunt in Kokstad, who may have been advising Lily on travel.
3. Of the Women's Hostel.

The Organizer, Non-European Section,
N.U.C., Durban.

Dear Madam,

I hoped that by the end of March or by this time I would be
right in school. Your last letter indeed worried me. You seem
to be getting a little estranged. When I wrote to you for the
first time I was telling you the honest fact by saying that I'm
a helpless orphan though anxious of education.

How can I show you the grief which overwhelms me? Even
this end I had been trying my level best to gain help. Do n't
think that I shall be your eternal worry or burden. What I wish
for is passing the Senior Certificate Examination this year.

The advisory friend has promised me some help when I'm
post matric.[1] Help during the time I'm in matric will be adequate
on your part. I had been advised to ask for help to you as early
as possible – and then I did ask you though you did not
answer my first letters. I have been ensured that you like
education and that you are a helpful lady.

Just think of the condition and grief I am in. I acquiesced
finding work to support myself because I know that success
comes to those who work for it. Then I wish I could get in
school as early as possible.

All along I had been hoping to be called by you as early
as possible. If you new how being an orphan is, you would
understand how life is for me. Many choose running away and
despairing everything – and that is common even to men. I
myself do n't want doing that since I'm a girl and that would
doom the rest of my life. I do n't want to go into any detail.

The second worry is the Matron's note. See it yourself. Is

1. This may refer to Lily's 'pen-friend', Alpheus Ndhlovu, at that time a
law student in Cape Town and later a barrister, who suggested she get
in touch with Mabel Palmer. The 'Penfriends' columns of the African press
were a popular medium for educated young Christian men to make contact
with educated young women at this time. Indeed as early as 1885 Elijah
Makiwane, a prominent member of the Eastern Cape elite, addressing the
Native Education Association, advocated penfriendship as a means whereby
Christian men find suitably literate wives. (*Imvo Zabantsundu*, 26 January
1885. I am grateful to Pallo Jordan for this reference.)

there no other place. Send me the fare. I'll mend everything there. Please do sympathise with me in reality.

I am, Yours truly,
Lily P. Moya

P.S. I'm writing the Matron the second letter but do n't wait that she replies me. Our magistrate can have no help unless if there were scholarships. There are none at all especially for students who are in matric. I have tried my best to ask for that scholarship but to no avail. 'The Same'

University of Natal, Durban.
14th April, 1949

Miss Lily Moya,
Box 30, Umtata.

Dear Miss Moya,

I am sorry that the reply from the Matron of the Women's Hostel was so disappointing, but perhaps it is just as well.

I have been making further enquiries from one of the Bantu Research Workers in the University of Natal, a man of much experience of native life in Durban,[1] and he tells me that he thinks it would be most undesirable that you should go to the Women's Hostel.[2] It does not appear to be a suitable place for a girl like yourself, and he could not suggest any other place where you could stay in Durban. So I am afraid we shall have to give that idea up.

I am considering what else could be done, but it is also uncertain and I do not know whether I could get the necessary support in some plans I have for you, so I would rather not say

1. This was Dr Selby Ngcobo, a prominent African academic in Natal, who had himself been helped to get social work training by Mabel Palmer in the 1930s. Born in 1909, he was educated at Adams, Fort Hare, and the Universities of Natal and Yale. At this time, he was in the Economics Department in the University of Natal and active politically. (See T. Karis, G. Carter and G. Gerhart, *From Protest to Challenge* [Stanford, California, 1977], vol. IV, 112.) Today Dr Ngcobo is economic adviser to the KwaZulu government.
2. For the reasons, see MP to NC, 14.4.49.

anything about it for the time being. But I will not forget you, and as soon as I can get something arranged, I will let you know.

You are, as a matter of fact, very much on my conscience, and I would feel myself very much to blame as an older woman who has been fairly successful in the field of education if I neglected your appeal. You can depend upon it that I will not do so if I can find any way of helping you. But you must have patience. It is never an easy thing to help a young woman in your position, and it is particularly difficult to do so in South Africa.

In the meantime, would you like some books? I could always send you some books which you could study yourself. Let me know the names of one or two books that you particularly want to read. I might give them to you or more probably I would just lend them to you for the time being. That at all events would make me feel that you were not wasting your time.

My Native friend recommends that I should write to the Native Commissioner at Umtata about you, and I am doing that immediately, and I am also turning over other plans in my mind.[3] But I reiterate that you must have patience, and that I will do everything I can to help you.

Yours sincerely,
Mabel Palmer

University of Natal, Durban
14th April, 1949

The Native Commissioner,
Umtata.

Dear Sir,

I am the Organizer of the Non-European classes of the University of Natal, and apparently I have achieved some amount of publicity among the Bantu people as one who is willing to help members of the Bantu race who are anxious to get an education.

---

3. Mabel was thinking of writing to her friends and to the Durban Branch of the South African Association of University Women in the hope of raising money. See her letters of 17.6.1949.

Bishop Bransby Key, the first missionary among the Mpondomise in Tsolo district who established St Cuthbert's Mission.

St Augustine's Church on the Inxu River built by Bishop Key.

'A spinning wheel and how to use it'; a useful aid to filling the 'somewhat dangerous time between the completion of a girl's schooling and her marriage. St Cuthbert's Mission.'

Workers and boarders at Gibson's Boarding School, St Cuthbert's Mission. Father Callaway is the tall figure in the centre, Archdeacon Gibson stands with arms folded at the left and Miss Blyth stands at the right.

A Transkei rural school, *c.* 1942.

Singing lesson at a Transkei school.

Snapshot of an unidentified girl. This picture was found among Mabel Palmer's papers and may well be the one Lily promised to send her.

A Transkei homestead. The Moya family home looked very like this.

In New York in the late 1920s.

Sibusisiwe Makhanya.

As Lily would have known her.

Mabel Palmer.
The photograph
is inscribed
'F. M. MacDonald
with love from
Mabel Palmer,
Durban, 30 March 1947'.

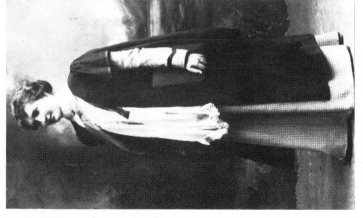

Mabel Atkinson in 1900
in her graduation gown.

I have had a series of very pathetic letters from a Lily Moya who gives her address as P.O. Box 30, Umtata. She represents herself as an orphan in charge of a guardian who is not interested in her, and is not prepared to help her in her desire for further education. I gather she is only about 15 or 16 years old. She enquires if I could admit her to the classes of the University of Natal, but she is much too young, and has not yet passed her matriculation examination, but the letters are very well expressed giving me the impression of a young thing straining at the leash with desire for some training to fit her to take part in the life outside a native location.[1]

When I remember the many people who helped me in years gone by to get the education which has enabled me to lead what has on the whole been a happy and successful life, I feel that I cannot shut my ears to her appeal.[2]

But on consulting Mr Selby Ngcobo, one of the Bantu Research Workers in the University of Natal, he advises me to write to you on the subject, first of all to find out if the girl's story corresponds to the facts, and secondly to advise me as to whether there is anything I can do to help her. I did think of asking her to come to Durban, putting her in the Girl's Hostel, helping her to get work, and then arranging for her to take classes at the M.L. Sultan Technical Institution, but I have learnt since that the Women's Hostel in Durban is by no means a well-managed place, and that it would be most unsuitable as a place of residence for an innocent young girl.

I have now been wondering whether it would be possible to get her into any of the good native secondary schools, such as Adams or Inanda,[3] but I should have to ask help from my friends in collecting special funds for this, and it seems desirable that I should first have some corroboration of the girl's story. I should be very much obliged if you could find out if the facts are as she states them and whether she appears to be a girl of whom it would be worth while to spend a good deal of

1. Mabel seems to be using the word interchangeably with 'native reserve' — i.e. those areas of land set aside for African occupation. By this time, the term 'location' was used more frequently in an urban context.
2. See Introduction, p.8.
3. Inanda was the 'sister' school to Adams, both having been founded by the American Board of Missions.

money in order that she might attain her aim. In England such a girl would almost certainly win a scholarship from a primary to a secondary school, and then go on to the University.

I should be infinitely obliged for your help in this matter.

I am,

Yours very truly,

Dr Mabel Palmer

Office of the Magistrate, Umtata
27th April 1949

Dr Mabel Palmer,
Organizer, Non-European Section,
University of Natal, Durban.

Dear Madam,

re: Lily Moya

With reference to your letter of the 14th instant – I wish to inform you that I have investigated the case of the above-named girl and found the facts to be mainly as stated by her. According to the Principal of the St. John's College she failed her Senior Certificate last year having obtained no higher symbol than 'G' in all the subjects.

She will be 16 years old in August next and I do not consider that she ought to be sent to a city like Durban or Pietermaritz-burg.[1] She lives with her aunt in the Tsolo district where her guardian, her late father's brother, also resides. He states that he cannot afford to put her to school, having a family of his own.

As Lily is still very young I suggested to her that she looks for employment for the balance of 1949 and reapply at the beginning of 1950.

Yours obediently,

MAGISTRATE – UMTATA

1. The dangers of urban life for young girls are a recurring theme amongst administrators, missionaries and African parents in 20th century South Africa – see Introduction, pp.23,31 for a discussion.

The Secretary,
The Non-European Section, N.U.C.,
Durban.

Dear Madam,

Yours latest received. Contents well notified and greatly encourageous. I've been called by the Native Commissioner here at Umtata. He has given me no better plan than yours. I must say it out, because he has forbidden me from leaving Umtata and said that the only plan he gives me is that I should find work here at Umtata and then apply earlier to St. John's College as a day scholar. I'm still too young to go to Durban, a very disagreeable place and I must n't worry myself – there is still a long time infront of me.

On that day, 26th April, I also went to ask the St. John's Principal Teacher to admit me in as a day scholar student, he agreed but after talking this over with the Warden, the latter said that it is too full.[1] I made a mistake by applying to the Principal Teacher at first. The Boarding master said that a case like mine occured last year with the same result. The Warden hates that the Principal Teacher should admit children without his consent at first, even if they have to be day scholars.

What I want to do is Corresponding this year if I can get some-one to pay for the tuition – at a session's period. I've posted two letters to two of these Corresponce Colleges, to choose the better from them. I have asked their tuition and if I could take the only subjects I've failed but sure to get an exemption in matric at the end of the year.

When you answer me also explain to me this and give me your real opinion on this. Don't be mislead to your consideration which you said you'll do in silence, by this letter. Tell me your decision when you write me.

---

1. Lily was clearly trying to get back to school after failing the matriculation examination for the first time at the end of 1948. She was noted in the reports for that year as 'difficult' – which may account for the Warden's reluctance to re-admit her. For a discussion of the meaning of 'difficult', see Epilogue, p.205.

Thanks I give to you for what you have promised to do for me, sending books, cannot be verbally described. Only Him who knows how thankful I am to you. When answered by the Secretary and Registrar of the Correspondence College I'll tell you what they say or enclose the letters in for you.

Books I'd like you to send me are 'King Lear' (a play by Shakespeare) 2. 'Jane Eyre' 3. 'Admirable Chrichton'.[2] Can be glad if you give me too their summaries.[3] I shall tell you the other books later, which I would like to read for pleasure.

You will not mind neh? answering me always. I confide in your advice and hope for your sincere consideration to all I write you.

Can be very glad if you correct my English errors and tell me when I'm getting worse or ameliorating.

With Greetings,

I am,

Yours truly,

Lily P. Moya

Use the above address. Not the previous. I'll tell you when to change it. 'The same'

Note in Mabel Palmer's handwriting
Adam's College fees £20 and another £20 in books, travelling and clothes.

---

2. As Sylvia Vietzen has remarked, there is something 'incongruous, yet irredeemably human' about this exchange of books. In fact, it was not quite as bizarre as it perhaps seems. As already indicated, Lily came from a long tradition of literacy, and these books were the set books for the Cape Senior Certificate examination, which had the same syllabus for black and white, rural and urban schools. Lily consistently misspelt 'Crichton' as 'Chrichton'.
3. Matriculation students in South Africa place a heavy reliance on published summaries of their set books.

The Secretary, The Non-European Section, N.U.C.,
Durban.

Dear Madam,

It disappoints me too severely when you do n't reply me. I really do n't know what to do now. I thought your answer to my letters would come earlier so that this time I would be busy with studies, I mean with reading the books.

Pardon me, if I've annoyed you in any case with my previous letter, to you. I also who ask you to correct my errors.

You said you would consider what to do about me, I hope then you've not forgotten your promise, and please after your conclusion write me I beg you.

It seems to me as if there is this person who always desuades you from helping me, if there is really any-one desuading you, please pay a deaf ear to that person's unphilanthropic advice.

The books I earnestly need are:

        1. King Lear
        2. Admirable Chrichton
        3. Essays of To-Day
        4. Queene Victoria
   and 5. Living Tradition (Poems)
   and 6. 'Jane Eyre'

You may not worry yourself about 'Jane Eyre' for the present moment I have finished reading it. I found it in the Native Public Library. Had it (Library) not been so narrow I would look for the rest of the books I need and read them.

I can be very glad if you can answer this letter of mine at your earliest possible. You may not say what you think to do for me if you have n't yet finished considering the matter. But, please send me the books.

Let me not expatiate,

                  With greetings, from
                  Yours sincerely,
                  Lily Moya

The Welcome Home, Umtata.
14/6/49

The Secretary,
The Non-European Section, N.U.C.,
Durban.

Dear Madam,

I'm really stranded. You seem to have completely withdrawn from giving me any help. I am puzzled. I cannot tell whether you are still considering my state of affairs as your promise in your last letter or you have been completely been desuaded by your advisers, against helping me.

There is no painful switch than the one you have threshed me with, not replying my letters. It is too difficult for me to guess, what causes you to suddenly change your mind against me.

Anyway − I do n't fully claim you as my adviser, but, you have taught me to trust in you, in your last letter.

Promise me this, will you please take me in your school, Adams College if I've struggled to pass the Senior Certificate Examination which may be a Cape or National Exemption one? It may-be next year or next year but one (1950 or 1951). Please I urgently ask for your reply to this particular note I write you.

All along I shall be expecting for yours, but please try, though you may be too busy and occupied, to give me an early reply, since I may perhaps be moving away in few weeks or days to seek work which may give me better earnings to help me to buy few articles such as clothing materials and so on.

Let me not expatiate.

So, Best greetings and love,
from
Lily Patience Moya

Natal University College, Durban
17th June 1949

The Magistrate,
Umtata

Dear Sir,

I have to thank you very much for your kindness in interesting yourself, at my request, in the case of Lily Moya.

I had not realised that she was only 15 years of age and I quite agree with you that she ought not to be taken away from home at that age, except perhaps to attend some recognised native boarding school of high standing.

I am trying to raise funds to send her to Adams College next year, but I do not know whether I shall be successful.

Thanking you again for your kind action in reference to my application for information.

I am,
Yours faithfully,
(Dr) Mabel Palmer

24 Clair Avenue, Durban.
17th June 1949

Mrs. Wood,
Chairman, Durban Branch,
S.A. Assn. of University Women.

Dear Mrs. Wood,

I do not know if you remember the case of Lily Moya which I mentioned to you. She is a little native girl of 16 years of age who lives near Umtata, and who is burningly anxious to continue her education. She is an orphan and her native guardian does not feel he can afford to send her away to school.

I have made enquiries about the cost of keeping her at Adams for a year and it would approximately amount to £50 in all; £20 for fees and another £30 for books, travelling expenses and clothes. Do you think your branch could do anything towards helping this ambitious young woman? I would be pleased to contribute to a fund for sending her to Adams College in 1950.

I enclose for you a copy of her first letter to me. I subsequently wrote to the Magistrate at Umtata who confirms her story but refuses to allow her to leave her guardian's care till next year.

I hope very much that the Durban Branch may be willing to give her some help.

Yours sincerely,
(Dr) Mabel Palmer

University of Natal, Durban
17th June 1949

Mrs. N.E. Whitehead,
Mount Victoria,
Box 21, Mooi River.

Dear Mrs. Whitehead,[1]

I wonder if you would be interested in the case of a poor native girl who has written to me begging for help in her education. I enclose a copy of her first letter to me. I have written to the Magistrate at Umtata who corroborates her story, but thinks that she ought not to leave the care of her guardian until 1950.

I should like, if possible, to send her to Adams College in 1950 which would cost about £30 for clothes, books, travelling expenses etc. and £20 for fees. I am asking the Durban Branch of the University Women's Association to help, and am prepared to contribute £5 a year myself, and I wondered if you would also care to give us a little help.

Things are going fairly well with us here and we expect to have our College next year at Wentworth.[2] This year the attendance in the Non-European classes has somewhat declined but I expect this is only a temporary setback. I miss your

---

1. Mrs N.E. Whitehead was a lady of philanthropic and liberal bent. She established the Non-European Progress Trust Fund, which gave £30 to Umbumbulu after her death in 1955.
2. Mabel is referring here to the opening of the Durban Medical School, with which she was very concerned. The University of Natal had recently acquired the Wentworth site on long lease from the Union Government

former kind contribution very much. Some members of the Indian community have promised to make it up and I expect that in the end they will do so, but reminding them over and over again is a very different matter from the prompt appearance of your cheque early each year!

Thank you again for all the kindnesses you have shown us in the past. I hope that you and all your family are well and that the grandchildren are progressing satisfactorily.

Yours very sincerely,
(Dr) Mabel Palmer

University of Natal, Durban
17th June 1949

Miss L.P. Moya,
The Welcome Home, Umtata

Dear Miss Moya,

You really must not become so impatient if you do not hear from me immediately. I am a very busy woman with a great deal to do for my own students, and it is only because your first letter appealed to me that I was willing to interest myself in your case. When I learnt from the Native Commissioner that you were only 15 and had not done well in your Senior Certificate last year, I realised that he was quite right in saying that you should not leave Umtata, and that anything beyond sending you books of which I have copies myself, there is nothing I can, or ought, to do for you until next year. I will try to get some of the books to you as soon as possible, but I do not know what you mean by item 4 – 'Queen Victoria'. There are a great many books about Queen Victoria and you must give me more details. Is it Lytton Strachey's Queen Victoria? King Lear and Jane Eyre I can send you immediately. I am only *lending* them, and will

---

through the intervention of General Smuts and the Provincial Administrator, D.G. Shepstone. The Union government had taken the buildings over from the British who had erected them during World War Two. The Alan Taylor Hall of Residence for black (mainly medical) students was established at Wentworth and classes for first and second year black medical students were held on the premises (Brookes, *A History of the University of Natal*, 86–7).

enclose little slips for you to sign and you must send these back to me at once, and return the books towards the end of the year. I may put in one or two other books that I think may interest you.

I certainly approve of your attitude that you should complete your matriculation or Senior Certificate by correspondence, though if you only got 'G' in all the subjects, as I am informed by the Umtata Magistrate, you will need to work very hard. You need to be careful about the correspondence colleges, as some of them are very poor indeed, but the University Correspondence at Pretoria [1] (though I am not sure that this one does pre-matriculation work) and the Rapid Results College in Mentieth House, Smith Street, Durban are both reliable. You might let me see them as soon as you have the answers from the correspondence colleges. I might, though I make no promises, be able to help you with the fees. For next year I have a plan for you in mind, but as I am not at all sure whether I shall be able to carry it out, I prefer to say nothing of it in the meantime.

I can only end by repeating what I have said before. I will not forget about you, but you must not expect me to arrange things in a hurry nor to answer your letters immediately. There are many people who have stronger claims on my attention and action than you yourself.

Yours sincerely,
(Dr) Mabel Palmer

1. Mabel was presumably referring to the University of South Africa or UNISA, which offers degree courses to both black and white through correspondence. For a very large number of Africans, part-time study through UNISA — and, at high school level, other correspondence colleges — was and still is the only route to upgrading their education. Many of the schools offering correspondence courses were fly-by-night organisations taking advantage of the black demand for education, but offering very little of real value.

Dr Sophie Kaplan Jackson,[1]
51 Grosvenor Court, Durban
June 20th 1949

Dear Dr Palmer,

Am in receipt of your letter of 17th June, for which many thanks.

I shall bring this matter to the notice of Members at the forthcoming General Meeting on Thursday, 23rd. and let you know if the Durban Branch[2] is willing to do something for this girl.

Yours sincerely,
Sophie Jackson

The Welcome Home, Umtata.
22/6/49

Dear Madam,

Many thanks for yours I received yesterday. I thought you'd never write me again, for a reason I could not guess. You've really relieved me a great deal.

I'm hoping for the next year. I'm really happy that though you are too busy you would not forget me, I also do realise that you cannot trust one you've never seen better than those you are acquainted with.

There is not much for me to say to you other than expressing my hearty thanks to you for your friendship. I hope that some day I may to see you personally.

I did not get 'G' in all subjects. Of course I got it in two subjects and I'm really ashamed of it but I could not help since the place at which I stayed to do my schooling last year especially was really unfavourable. I would go to school without meals and come back and work hard after school. There was no time for studies and walked a long way to school. It sounds funny and incredible but is perfect truth.

1. Apparently the Secretary of the Durban branch of the South African Association of University Women.
2. Of the South African Association of University Women.

Let me not expatiate on this, it makes me to sob.
Greetings and love,

Yours sincerely,
Lily P. Moya

P.S. I can be glad if you would not call me 'Miss Moya' but write 'Dear Lily or Patience' not 'Dear Miss Moya'
'The Same'

P.O. Box 30, Umtata
9.7.49

My dear Dr Palmer,

Many thanks for your letter and parcel. It is very kind of you. I cannot express my thanks to you verbally. I wish you do n't get tired of me.

Oh! I understand that you must be very busy being a Doctor[1] and a Secretary for Non-European Section, of all the Natal Province, and it is really kind of you to care for me a foreigner whom you've never seen and who is in no way connected and neither is related to you.

I must repeat it is very kind of you and teaches me a good carrier[2] to be taken by myself all the time I'm alive.

. The Corresponce Colleges are no good they do n't entitle one to any University which means to say such a Senior Certificate is useless.[3]

Had you some work in your clinic or so I would gladly come to while away this session, but, I also wish writing the Senior Certificate Examination this year and see how much I have done with the books you've given me.

In spite of your business I become happy when you reply me not that I do n't sympathise with you, but I like receiving a letter from you.

1. Understandably, Lily thought that Mabel was a medical doctor. Mabel Palmer had been granted an honorary doctorate by the University of South Africa in 1947.
2. i.e. career.
3. A reference to Mabel's letter of 17.6.1949.

I wish you do n't get tired of me. I'm about to finish reading
'King Lear'.

My greetings and love,

Yours sincerely,
Lily M. Moya

Handwritten note attached to the letter of 9.7.49
Send particulars to (illegible)
Apply Clem. Woods
   Mr Ellis Brown
   Mrs Erasmus Brown
     for contribution[1]

P.O. Box 30, Umtata
30/8/49

My dearest Dr Palmer,

It makes me very glad writing you this letter. As the year
draws near to the end I really become more happy. My heart
is really beating with curiosity. I'm quite anxious to know what
provision you've put me for next year.

Early in July after I had written you, thanking you very
much for your dear patronage, there came a certificate stating
that I failed in last year's final Exams and passed only in *three
subjects* and in the *aggregate*.[2] I wish I had passed at least four,
I would have had a supplementary privelege, which I'm sure I
would have passed it by now.

'The Secretary' for the 'Educational Department', 'Exam
Branch' at Cape Town in reply to my letter asking him for an
Examination Entrie Form, that could not I be exempted from
the subjects I passed, he said that as I failed more than two
subjects I will have to write the whole Exams again, and he

1. This note is further evidence of Mabel's energetic efforts on Lily's
behalf. Again she had little success with these wealthier members of
Natal's bourgeoisie.

2. According to the matriculation results for 1948, she obtained an 'E'
grade in the December examination, 41.2% in the September school tests.
I am grateful to Rosalie Kingwell of Umtata for a transcript of these results.

sent the Form, although I'm not sure whether I shall have the chance or luck of writing the Exams.

On the 11th inst. I was called by the Principal Teacher of a near by [school a] few miles from home, Ncambele Secondary School to act as a substitute for an ill teacher. He was forced by the Manager of Schools and especially the Inspector to find a substitute, they could n't find anyone fit but somehow he got knowledge of me and I was called. I did not know the reason for my call. It was great shock to me, that I should teach. The Principal Teacher was quite amazed – he did n't know that I was so small, indeed, the students are very big in that school.[3] I had to teach Xhosa, Phy[4] & Hygiene, Biology – Form A, B & C, take girls in drill, and singing B & C.

Just you imagine how I nearly lost my senses, how I shivered from toe to hair when I found myself standing infront of such big students, very old indeed for such standards.

The Principal Teacher after addressing me to the students and staff, and telling them that they must n't despise me, told me that any-one who is bully especially the 'Form B's' or does n't do work properly must be reported to him and he would give them a very severe corporal punishment. I must punish all those who are disobedient.

We co-operated with the students, merely because they were afraid of the Principal Teacher and that some of them know me they were my classmates and senior by age.

On the following week I was greatly released by convalesce of the teacher. I had been told to make a record of the work I had done, which work they admired and praised.

That is some experience I have undergone for three days, which I fear very much, though the ill teacher said, 'practise makes perfect'.

What would you have done if you would have been myself. Would you have gone to the classrooms or ran back home? This incidence brought a great change to this prolonged monotonous life.

Please, send me a book, the 'Admirable Chrichton'. I have 'Victoria' by (Lytton Strachey). I have finished reading 'Queen

3. See Introduction, p.27.
4. i.e. Physiology and Hygiene.

Victoria', King Lear and 'Jane Eyre' though I have n't a copy of my own for the latter. I'm beggining *'Living Tradition'*. Correspondence Colleges are very dear for me particulary. I do n't think, I may say I cannot afford to pay such amounts, and they are based for the National Education and not Provincial one which is highly critised but highly educated people. They suggest that I'm not fit for such a privete Education. Please, tell me your own opinion and suggestion. I shall follow your own precious advice. I want no 'too many cooks' because they will 'spoil the broth'.[5]

I shall try by all means to send you a snap shot[6] of mine and please will you send me yours. Tomorrow is my birthday.

With all my greetings,

Yours sincerely,
Lily

P.S. I hope for your earliest reply.

London
5.9.49

Dear Dr. Palmer,

Your letter and the copy were forwarded here. Just now I can do nothing about that native girl as you will see we are away from home and will not be back till October.

I do not yet know what the position will be due to this import control.[1] I hope the Indian community will make up

5. She obviously means having too many advisers.
6. There is unfortunately no record of Mabel's receiving such a snapshot, though it is possible that an unlabelled photograph in her collection is of Lily.

1. Foreign exchange and import controls had become 'a politico-economic necessity' to the Nationalist Party to curb the drain on foreign exchange after their victory in 1948 and to stem the 'upsurge of imports' once the log-jam of the war years on the import of both capital and consumer goods had been broken. The initial response of manufacturers in South Africa to the import controls was one of outrage. Although Horwitz points out, probably correctly, that 'no major manufacturing group and no heavily capitalized undertaking from 1948 in South Africa was delayed in its capital-expansion programme by other than a few additional meetings with more rarefied levels of hierarchical authority...', smaller concerns

that amount as I think they should do so.[2]

I am hoping to see Peg Ballinger[3] soon and to hear all the latest news. We don't like what we have managed to glean at all.[4]

With kindest regards,

Yours very sincerely,
M. Whitehead

South African Association of University Women
415 Manning Road, Durban
9. ix. '49

Dear Dr. Palmer,

At a general meeting of the Branch held yesterday, the question of Lily Moya was put forward for discussion.

With regard to her letter, two of the headmistresses present, agreed that it was not of matriculation standard and also that her statement that she 'had been a candidate for the Senior Certificate' was somewhat ambiguous.[1]

Other relevant factors pointed out, were that the help required would be for more than one year and this would be an expensive undertaking for the Branch which is struggling so hard for

---

were often adversely affected: hence apparently Mrs Whitehead's anxieties. (R. Horwitz, *The Political Economy of South Africa* [London, 1968], 283, 288.)

2. Contributions towards the non-European section of the University of Natal.

3. Margaret Ballinger, born Margaret Hodgson, in Glasgow, 1894, came to South Africa at the age of 10. An historian by training, she lectured at the University of Witwatersrand, until her election in 1937 to the House of Assembly as one of the three African representatives (for the Eastern Cape) under the 1936 Native Representatives' Act. A forceful and courageous parliamentarian, she was re-elected until the abolition of even this modicum of representation by the Nationalist government in 1960. She was a founder and initial president of the South African Liberal Party, and thus, like Mabel, part of the 'liberal establishment'.

4. The latest news about the political situation in South Africa. This letter reflects the anxieties of English-speaking South Africans in the early days of National Party rule.

1. The statement was probably deliberately ambiguous, in the light of her failure in the examination; the true failure, however, was that of the Branch which clearly had no conception of the nature of Lily's achievement.

the Isie Smuts Fellowship Fund.[2] The question of creating a precedent was also mentioned.

Under these circumstances, the meeting felt it could not support the request and suggested that perhaps if you contacted Senator Brooks,[3] he would interest himself in the case. Being a resident of Umtata, she would not come under the Natal Schools jurisdiction and perhaps Fort Hare[4] would be a more suitable goal for Lily.

Thanking you,

Yours sincerely,
Peggy Lewin

Handwritten note attached to letter of 9.9.49

Rang up Dr Allan Taylor.[1] He says there is no restriction of height for nurses and he would be prepared to admit Lily Moya if she has passed J.C. or equivalent. Write to her.

2. A scholarship fund established for white women in the name of the late wife of General Smuts.
3. Senator Edgar H. Brookes, who had been headmaster of Adams (1934–45), and who was one of the four indirectly elected African representatives in the South African Senate, from 1937 until 1953. A founder member of the South African Liberal Party, and a key member of the liberal establishment, Mabel would have known him through their joint interest in Adams, and the Institute of Race Relations. Prof. Brookes taught history and political science at the University of Natal between 1953 and 1962. He died in 1979. For his autobiography, see Edgar Brookes, *A South African Pilgrimage* (Johannesburg, 1977).
4. i.e. the African University College of Fort Hare, founded as the South African Native College in 1916, near Alice in the Eastern Cape. By mid-century it had an enviable reputation as an educational institution for Africans from southern, central and East Africa. In 1959 control of Fort Hare was taken over by the Minister of Bantu Education; its multi-racial and multinational character was destroyed, and its student intake largely confined to Xhosa and Mfengu students. A number of its leading staff members, including Professor Z.K. Matthews, resigned in protest.

1. Dr Alan Boardman Taylor, then Dean of Natal's newly formed Faculty of Medicine, the precursor of the Durban Medical School, and head of the McCord Zulu Hospital in Durban. A medical missionary of the American Zulu Mission he had come to Durban in 1922 at the instance of Dr McCord, who had hoped then to establish medical training for African doctors. It took nearly forty years for his dream to reach fruition. Alan Taylor was a key figure in the founding of the Medical School in Durban, as was Mabel Palmer.

Miss Lily Moya,
P.O. Box 30, Umtata.

Dear Lily,

I hope you received the book I sent you for a birthday present,
'The Admirable Crichton'. I have been speaking about you to
Dr Allan Taylor of McCord's Hospital, Durban. He says that, if
you have the equivalent of the Junior Certificate (which I think
you must have as you were going forward to the Cape Senior),
he might be prepared to admit you to the Nurses' Training at
McCord's Hospital.[1]

You will be very lucky if this can be arranged as McCord's
is one of the best Bantu Hospitals in Durban. Will you please
write to him at once – Dr Allan Taylor, Superintendent McCord's
Zulu Hospital, McCord Road, Durban. Tell him about your
educational qualifications and your desire to be a nurse.[2] He
tells me he knows of no restriction with regard to height. Then
let me know what he says and whether there seems to be any
possibility of your being accepted for training at McCord's.

Three other things:- Firstly, I am not a medical doctor. I have
what is called an honorary doctor's degree which was given me
largely because of the work that I have done in providing University Education for Non-Europeans; so I have no clinic or any
other office in which I could employ you.

Secondly, could you tell me what your religion is. I understand that it is possible to get admission for Catholic girls

1. McCord's Hospital was founded through the initiative of Dr J.B. McCord,
a medical missionary attached to the American Zulu Mission, in 1909, in
the face of bitter settler opposition. In the 1920s, McCord was in the forefront of those pioneering training for African nurses, and an ardent advocate of paraprofessional training for African health workers. (For the
history of the hospital and McCord's plans, see J.B. McCord, *My Patients
were Zulus* [London, 1946], 145–58, 201.)
2. Lily's expression of interest in nursing was very much a passing fancy;
as her letter to Mabel of 12.10.49 reveals, it was not a profession that
attracted her, although it was one of the most prestigious and better paid
occupations open to educated African women at this time. (See H. Kuper,
'Nurses', in L. Kuper, *An African Bourgeoisie* [New Haven and London,
1965], 216–233.)

fairly easily to the Secondary School at Mariannhill.[3]

Thirdly, I was very much interested in your letter about your teaching experiences. I think you really write in a very lively and amusing way. Now do you think you could do me a short paper on 'The Life of a Native Girl in a Native Reserve'? You do, I think, live in a Native Reserve, or if not wherever else you live.[4] Do not make it too grand. Write it just in the same way as you would write a letter to me. Imagine yourself telling me all about the way you live, the people you meet, the things you have to do. Make it about two thousand words long and then I might try to have it printed somewhere. I hope you will be able to do this. I hope also that the arrangement with McCord's will come off because it would be the very thing for you.

I have been trying to get some money to send you to one of the Bantu Boarding Schools next year but people are not in a very generous mood at present and I have not found it easy.

With best wishes,

Yours very sincerely,
(Dr) Mabel Palmer

P.O, Box 30, Umtata
2/10/49

The Organizer, The Non-European Section,
Natal University College, Durban.

Dear Dr Mabel Palmer,

Your silence impresses me severely, in so much that patience fails me. This idle living is not endurable physically as well as spiritually. I'm withering as well as desponding. You will kindly excuse me for my desultoriness. I cann't help it.

In all things combined I'm praying very hard that you do not forget me. All my hopes are diverted to you. There is no other person from whom I can get help other than you.

3. This was the St Francis Training College and High School at Mariannhill, a Trappist mission settlement. At this time it had an established reputation for 'industrial training', and ran schools for girls and boys.
4. The Transkei was, at that time, a 'native reserve'; it is today a so-called 'independent homeland'. It is startling to find Mabel Palmer, so widely regarded as an 'authority' on 'native life' so vague on the subject. (See Introduction, p.12.)

I think it highly expedient devoting myself to education as there is no powerful possession exceeding it (except divine). Let no-one or nothing impede you from helping me as from next year.

In the real sense of speaking I'm attenuating with the ending of the year because I do not know what will become of me next year. I'm really anxious to be in Durban. There is no good of my staying here. Opportunities will fail me but I must stay and wait for the Exams, and leave after them as early as possible in December.

Do not get tired of me and of my monotous, egotistic and solemn letters.[1] Kindly overlook my errors and desultoriness.

I hope to hear from you very soon,

I am,
Yours sincerely,
Patience Moya

P.S. I wish taking a B.Sc Degree Course after Matric or D.Sc.

('The Same')

Note in Mabel Palmer's hand
Wait till Oct 12 — for answer to crossing letter.

P.O. Box 30, Umtata.
12/10/49

The Organizer, The Non-European Section,
Natal University College, Durban.

My dear Dr Mabel Palmer,

Ever so many thanks for yours. It is both discouring and encouraging. The encouraging part, about Marianhill School, and, is it a Secondary School? Though I am not a Catholic I can assure you that I have some hope. I belong to the Anglican Church. The discouraging part, about the unwillingness of people in giving help.

---

1. One wonders whether these were the epithets being applied to Lily by her teachers and relatives at this time.

May I have hope for next year? of attending school? Is it possible that I may stay home next year while others, some quite bigger than I go to school? My heart really aches. I do not want thinking too much on this, but I cann't avoid it as it comes on automatically.

Nursing is not a profession I like very much though I like Nurses. I fear the solitary, sad scene of the Hospital, such as mourning of broken and burnt, dying people. I do not think when I am a Nurse I would ever have a sleep.

I do not mean I shall never be a Nurse but when compelled by unfavourable circumstances such as financial embarrasment and when utterely having no means of going to school, but even then I do not think I can be admitted in any Hospital before reaching the age of eighteen years.

Yes, I passed the Junior Certificate Examinations and had been a Senior Certificate Candidate. I shall soon write to Dr A. Taylor accordingly (apply).

I must thank you very sincerely for the birthday present, though it has not yet arrived. May you be always friendly to me. Correct me of, and overlook my errors.

I'm very sorry for not producing you a good draft to the 'Life of an African girl'.[1] I have not been a good traveller or very observant to such a subject, you will see little of my experience only based to what our people say of our girls and what we ought to do, to be preserved divinely devoted and single minded, expecting ourselves to be the future mother's, the examples to be admired and to be selfrespective of ourselves.

We are frequently mislead by minor misdeeds. We never use our intelligence. We are flying for only outside admiration, our actions are rot, revealing our internal impurity.

We have a thrilling audacity to do evil. We forget the meaning of the word 'girl', that a girl should be preserved. We make people believe that civilization came with evil. Yes, we are people surrounded by stumbling-blocks, things which look inviting. Reasoning power is failing us. All malecious advertisements we happen to come into visual contact — become our essential striving for so long as it is externally well attired.

1. For the significance of what follows, see Introduction, pp.21–25.

Our conscious and real honest aims fail us. We live only for the present but not for the future. Sometimes we are given wrong teaching by people we happen to stay with. We are only advised to marry and as we grow we think of nothing else but marry.

We have natural enemies, the ruffians who would always show violence to us, who think themselves better, who had or are workers in towns, because they are used to girls come in towns who have no self-respect.[2]

I am sorry that I am not as eloquent as to express what I mean of how the state of position our girls, who have themselves brought a curse of divorces on many women. A girl is to be preserved. To be always influential, religious, effective and self-respective.

I do not know whether I have drawn this as you would like it placed.

Yours very sincerely
Lily Moya

University of Natal, Durban
14 October, 1949

Miss Lily Moya,
P.O. Box 30, Umtata.

Dear Miss Moya,

Dr Palmer has had no reply to her letter of the 29th September nor any acknowledgement of the book 'The Admirable Crichton' which she sent you as a birthday present.

I am enclosing a copy of the letter in case you have not received it.

Yours sincerely,
SECRETARY

2. For the frequently disruptive effect on the women left behind of the return of young men from migrant labour see, for example, L. Clark and J. Ngobese, *Women without Men* (Durban, Institute for Black Research, 1975); D. Gaitskell, 'Wailing for Purity', op.cit. and C. Murray, *Families Divided* (Cambridge, 1981).

My dear Dr Mabel Palmer,

It is of pleasure for me to write you this short note. I wish to express my hearty thanks to you for the birthday present you sent me. It arrived later the letters I wrote you. Also I wish to inform you that I'm writing the Cape Senior Certificate,[1] asking for your prayers, will be finishing on the 6th December. You know it is a sort of trying because you know that I had not been coached in studies by any and it has been more difficult in set books which are all new.

You will always not put me in a dark corner of oblivion. I need not go into detail. At the present moment I'm feeling quite dry. There is not a single day I shall be free in writing this week and next week only, on Monday.

I'm not at home as you can note but address my letter with the above address. I hope to get the reply as soon as I finish writing.

With love from

Yours sincerely,
Lily

P.S. I hope you received the letter I wrote you.

My dearest Dr Mabel Palmer,

I am very glad to have this chance of writing you. I do not know what makes you so silent these days. Did you receive the two letters I have written you, excluding the one I wrote you in reply to the one you said I should write on the ('Girl Life' of Native)? I'm really worried now. It is a long time I have been waiting for yours.

In any case I return back the two books you lended to me. Hearty thanks for them. Again I must thank you for the three present books you gave me. I do not know how I should express my thanks to you but I hope God will thank you for me in a better way I cannot do myself.

1. For the second time.

Await the books in the following post or this.

I wish you a happy, happy Xmas and New Year, but please write me before these take place.

Devotedly yours obedient,

Patience Lily Moya

University of Natal, Durban.
4th January, 1950

Miss Lily Moya,
P.O.Box 30, Umtata

My dear Lily,

I am returning herewith the paper that you did for me on the 'Life of a Girl in a Native Reserve'.[1]

It is not really very good. It is much too general and gives too little detail, and I think it is a pity that you devote so much of it to describing the bad manners of some Zulu girls.[2] There are always a certain number of bad mannered girls everywhere.

Will you try it again and try to answer such questions as these:-

1. What is your earliest memory?
2. How were you treated as a very small child?
3. Is it true that Zulu children are very seldom punished?
4. What sort of toys did you have when you were very tiny?
5. When did your mother die, and what difference did it make to you?
6. In what ways are little girls say of seven treated differently to little boys say of seven years?
7. When did you first go to school?

I liked particularly the letter you wrote to me describing your experiences as a teacher. Can you not get a little more of that kind of touch into your article?

Tell me something about your teachers.

1. This letter is discussed in the Introduction on p.12.
2. As noted in the Introduction, it is really quite extraordinary that Mabel should have thought that Africans in the Transkei were Zulu. It is the equivalent of imagining that the Welsh live in Ireland.

Where did you get your books and how is it you are so fond of English books. Tell us about some of the books that you have read?

Imagine that you are writing to an English girl in Durban about the same age as yourself who wants to know in what way your upbringing is different to hers.

What sort of amusements do young adolescent girls have in Zulu Reserves? Do you often go to the Movies for instance? Do you go to dances?

Do not make it too long, about 1,000 words, and please write on one side of the page only. That is one of the first rules of a would-be journalist.

Well now, try it again, and if you can produce a lively and interesting account of how a girl grows up in a Zulu Reserve, I will see what I can do with it.

Let me know as soon as possible if you have passed matriculation or the equivalent, the Cape Senior. If you have not passed I will arrange to send you to school somewhere in Natal for a year, in order that you may complete your matriculation, but I cannot very well make arrangements for that while your matriculation results are still pending, so please let me know as soon as possible.

Hoping that 1950 will bring you a happier existence than you have known in the past.

> Believe me,
> Yours sincerely,
> (Dr) Mabel Palmer

> *Qutubeni School,*
> *St. Cuthbert's Mission,*
> *P.O. St. Cuthberts.*
> *1/2/50*

My dearest Dr Mabel Palmer,

I am very glad to have the chance of replying your letter of the 5th. Thanks very much for it. I have just received it because I had not been at home. I had been asked by my maternal Aunt to her place, and now she has left for Johannesburg.

You can see I am at the above school only for one quarter, I suppose. I have notified the 'Father Superior', that, I hope to

93

go back to school and finish my course at first. He said, well, if I can get means of attending school I may do so. I should not refuse such a luck.

So, please do not forget your promise that you would send me to school to complete the Matriculation Course. I shall arrive early next quarter because the 'Fathers'[1] refuse that I should leave now as I am the only teacher at the above school.

Do you know what kind of school this is? I mean to say it is a very hard job for me:- The school is newly established at a place where there was never a light of any sort of civilization. There is no church. The nearest one is a distance of five or more miles away. All people except the woman I stay with are proper heathens, I mean red people.[2] The nearest store is more than five miles away. Some of the children do not know what I mean by talking about the ball, cup, and many other simple and common things.

The place itself is surrounded by gigantic mountains. The country is stoney. It is as primitive as I think the old stories relate to us how the people were before 'Nongqwause'.[3] I never dreamt that there was still such a backward place.

The children have no manners at all. They have no discipline. Some spit in the school room. They are untidy. This morning I took them to the river to bathe. I mean the whole school of them. I tell them that a school child must look gay, smart, tidy and a disciplinarian, obedient etc. There are big girls and boys, bigger than I, some my size and some very small children now.

Can you guess how many children had I on the opening day, 23rd ultimo, only three, on Wednesday 25th, five. Do you know how many were on Friday, thirty-one, and today, are thirty-five children on roll.

My punishment is pinching them. They have improved a great deal. They know now counting in English up to ten, reading and

1. The Fathers of the Society of St John the Evangelist (S.S.J.E.) who ran St Cuthbert's Mission.
2. In the Eastern Cape, non-Christian Africans were (and in some areas still are) referred to as 'red people', because of the red ochre with which they daub themselves. The division between 'Red' and 'School' people is highly significant amongst the Xhosa. Clearly Lily uses the term with contempt.
3. For Nongqwause (or Nonqause) see Introduction, note 27.

writing the figures. They know reading and writing their vowels. I can command them to do certain but still few things in English. They know parts of their bodies and the parts of the room in English. They like games and singing, though they are still very bad in training their voices and in singing the right notes. Any-way, they are becoming better than toads in a pool.

Don't you agree with Brother Bourdon S.S.J.E. who said that I am doing a Missionary hard work.

Two very young children begged me to buy them dresses, so I gave them my old two dresses! The others are very anxious to have dresses and shirts and trousers. Some have given me materials to cut them their dresses and shirts. I have not refused. They are keeping me very busy mentally and physically you know and still spiritual. I pray for my children.

I am the only teacher in this school, but am an unaided teacher inspite of that work.

On the first day I came here I came with 'Father Superior' from St. Cuthberts' and two other people. There were many people (men) waiting us. I was introduced to them as their mistress and that I do not deserve the place they should treat me kindly etc.

Oh I shall relate you more news next time, during this short time I am not in Durban yet, and please kindly reply this letter at your earliest convinience. I have not heard anything about my results. I am afraid I have not come out through the Exams, besides, I am far away from Umtata: but I think I shall break up one week end for Umtata very soon, so as to know of my post etc.

Remember that you have promised to take me to school. You will upset my mind if you refuse because I am very much determined to attend any school in Natal you send me to. Be not mislead by my being at this Qutubeni School as a teacher, that is a matter of one quarter. Yes, if I had passed my Exams I would stay longer but staying with an unfinished course is senselessness or foolishness.

I am sending the composition very soon. Wait for it.

With fondest greetings,
Yours sincerely,
Lily P. Moya

P.S I am just in the black hole of Calcutta and I don't like it at all.

Qutubeni School
C/o Revd Father Superior
P.O. St Cuthbert's Mission,
Tsolo
23.2.50

My dear Dr Mabel Palmer,

I write this letter before getting a reply to the one I wrote you. I do not know what is keeping you. Perhaps it may be, you are waiting for the 'essay'.[1] I will be sending it very soon.

I mean to tell you I have not passed the Exams. You will not forget your promise, – sending me to one of your schools to complete this course. Remember that promises are to be fulfilled. If it had not been due to Father Superior giving notice, I would be glad to be in school there at Natal now.

Please write me.

With fondest greetings,
Yours sincerely,
Lily

Tsolo[2]
5.4.50

Dear Dr Mabel Palmer,

I wish to inform you my new address, as I hope you will write me more especially as you promised me with schooling.

I am at my mother's home – my uncle's place. Will stay here till something new occures for me, such as going to school or any other profession.

You will remember I wrote a letter at Qutubeni. The schools have been closed on the 31st ultimo. for 'Good Friday' etc. I made a notice in school,[3] hoping that you would fulfil your promise.

---

1. 'The Life of a Native Girl in a Native Reserve'. In fact, it seems as though Lily never rewrote it.

2. The full address has been omitted for reasons of confidentiality.
3. i.e. given notice to the school.

Kindly let me know all what is about and please reply this note at your earliest convenience.

With Greetings,
Yours sincerely,
Lily P. Moya

Umtata
20th May, 1950

My dear Dr Mabel Palmer,

I am so very glad to receive yours, as well as very sorry to get it so very late. You will then forgive me for replying it so very late.

How now? Didn't I tell you that I failed Std. X. Altogether, I have no means nor are there any available means for me to carry on my education, due to financial disabilities. The position is as I told you and there is no improvement at all.

I don't think I would have troubled you so much if I had any hopes of help anywhere else. I am quite desitute.

If you can just find me a school to learn and work that can be quite alright. I would work while learning.

All along, I had been patiently waiting for your final decision. Kindly help me.

With best wishes,
Yours sincerely,
Lily Moya

University of Natal, Durban
26th May, 1950

Mr. G.C. Grant,
Principal,
Adams College,
P.O. ADAMS MISSION

Dear Mr Grant,

Herewith a copy of Lily Moya's latest letter, in order that you may have some first hand information about her.

I am sending you also her first letter which I see was addressed to the Registrar, and later handed to me as dealing with the non-European students, also copy of letter from the Magistrate at Umtata.

I was struck with the lively and interesting way in which she writes in her apparently helpless position, and I gave her a definite undertaking to help her.

I understood that she was sitting again for the examination last November, and expected to hear how she had done in it; apparently, however, she did not sit, and was sometime in advising me of that fact.

I would be so much obliged if you could do something for her, I will be responsible for expenses up to £50. I hope I will be able to collect some of the money from friends of mine.

Thank you very much for your kind interest, and I hope that we will be able to give this girl a start in life.

I approached Dr Allen Taylor with regard to her entering a Nursing course, but by the time she had become set on an academic course, leading to teaching. She has actually done a certain amount of teaching in a Catholic school[1] not far from her home and she wrote me really quite an amusing account of how she had to cope with a class, almost all of whom were much bigger than herself.

Yours very sincerely,
(Dr) Mabel Palmer

Adams College
P.O. Adams Mission Station
Natal, South Africa
29th May, 1950

Dr. Mabel Palmer,
University of Natal, Durban.

Dear Dr Palmer,

I thank you for your letter of the 26th May concerning Lily Moya. I am writing to her, and if her papers are in order I

---

1. This was another of Mabel's lapses. The school was, of course, Anglican, and Lily had already told Mabel that she was not a Catholic.

shall advise that she come to us next term rather than wait for yet another term. I shall keep you informed.

With kind regards,

Yours sincerely,
G.C. Grant[1]
Principal

Adams College, Natal
29th May, 1950

Miss Lily P. Moya,
P.O. Box 30, Umtata.

Dear Madam,

I have been approached by Dr Mabel Palmer of Natal University on your behalf. I am writing therefore to request you to send me your qualification without delay so that I may advise Dr Palmer what I may be able to offer you. Let me know what examinations you have passed, and the symbols you have obtained in any external examination. I enclose a Form for you to fill in yourself, and one for you to have filled in by the Principal of your last school. Please reply as soon as possible.

Yours faithfully,
G.C. Grant
Principal

University of Natal, Durban
1st August, 1950

The Principal,
Adams College,
P.O. Adams Mission.

Dear Mr Grant,

I wonder if you have heard anything from Lily Moya.

You were good enough to say that you would get into touch with her and possibly arrange for her to be admitted this term.

1. G.C. Grant became the Principal of Adams in 1957. For his auto-biography, including his sojourn at Adams, see Jack (G.C.) Grant, *Jack Grant's Story* (Farnham, 1980).

99

As I shall be responsible for paying her fees it would be very kind of you if you would let me know how the matter stands at present?

I hear that the Vacation School[1] was a great success and that people who had never been present before were greatly impressed.

I hope you were not too tired after it and with kind regards to Mrs Grant and yourself,

I am,
Yours sincerely,
(Dr) Mabel Palmer

Adams College, Natal
4th August, 1950

Dr Mabel Palmer,
Box 1525, Durban.

Dear Dr Palmer,

I thank you for your letter of the 1st August concerning Lily Moya. I regret to say that I am unable to find in my files a letter from me to her, so it is possible that I did not write her. I therefore offer you my apologies for this oversight. At the same time I believe that I did write her. I shall write her now, and I trust that an answer will soon be forthcoming.

I am sorry that I missed you when you visited Adams during the Vacation Course. It went off very well I am glad to say, and your staff deserve every credit. I hope it will be possible for you to persuade Prof Ventris to come over and help you.

With kind regards,

Sincerely,
G.C. Grant

P.S. I enclose a copy of my letter to Miss Moya

1. This was probably the winter school at Adams initiated by Mabel Palmer in the 1930s for teachers and black part-time students in the non-European section of Natal University. (See Introduction, p.5.)

Miss Lily Moya,
Umtata.

Dear Miss Moya,

Dr Mabel Palmer, the Organizer of the Non-European Section of Natal University has kindly written to me on your behalf. She informs me that you desire to continue your studies, and that you would like to sit your Matriculation Examination. I am prepared to accept you as a student at Adams College, and I recommend you to come to us as soon as possible — the sooner the better.

As you have not been preparing the set books for this year it will not be possible for you to take the final examination in December, but if you have not fallen back too much in your studies and if you are prepared to work hard, then you should be able to take the examination next year. Let me know how soon I may expect you, and I shall forward you the concession form and the train fare if you are unable to find the money.

I await an early reply. Assuring you of my readiness to assist you and to avail myself of the kind offer of help which Dr Palmer has made — namely to pay your fees and other small incidental expenses.

Please do not delay in answering this letter.

Yours faithfully,
G.C. Grant
Principal

P.S. I enclose the Concession Forms

The Girl's Department, P.O. Adams College
[7/9/50][1]

My dear Dr Mabel Palmer,

With greatest pleasure I write you this letter of thanks.

1. The original reads 7/10/50, but this is clearly in error, for 7/9/50.

Both my joy and thanks cann't be meted.[2] Had I means of actional thanks[3] I would do great things for you. In all things combined I pray and hope that He would thank you for me, and to multiply the kindness you've done a many more times for you and to extend it to all connected with you in this wonderful, incredible sympathy.

Seeing that things were becoming worse, unbearable and torturous, I determined to leave, not understanding actually what I was doing and the result to be afterwards.[4]

They refused at Kokstad to give me a ticket for Natal, unless I could produce a ticket or concession form. Of course I couldn't wait for anything like a letter or so from you or the College as I noticed unhumane difficulties in front of me were more than bearable. I said to the Station Master I was going for Riverside the junction of the Cape and Natal. Think of that terrible risk! If the guards of the train could find it out, woe! would be unto me and how glad my enemies would have been. I would have been a topic and would have been pointed with a thumb.[5] At Riverside I took another ticket to Pietermaritzburg. Of course you had arranged for me there in Pietermaritzburg. I couldn't believe my eyes at all, when I arrived here and when I saw you too.

Can I see you sometimes? You haven't forgotten me at all. I would like to see you as frequently as possible. There is still some difficulty as I haven't got anything, such as bedding, uniform and books. Now I am placed at 'Pollet' dormetry.

The day I came I met 'Dean'[6] with other two European ladies. They were very kind to me and especially 'Dean'. She took me to her house where she gave me some nice food. It was really kind of her.

I am trying my best to cover up. Next year will do my utmost best in Form V. I suppose there are still more days in front for me to talk to and write you.

Greetings and Long live,

Yours faithfully,
Lily P. Moya

2. i.e. measured.
3. i.e. of showing her thanks 'in action'.
4. For an explanation, see LM to MP, 12.9.50.
5. She would have been a topic of malicious conversation, and people would have pointed at her.
6. The Dean of Women Students.

y

Mr Bomback,[1]
Adams College.

Dear Mr Bomback,

I am enclosing a cheque for £5 for the immediate needs of Lily Moya as I felt after I had left Adams on Monday that I ought perhaps not to expect Adams to purchase blankets etc. for her. If there is any surplus it can of course be applied to her fees.

She certainly is, in spite of her very quiet and shy exterior, a young woman of extraordinary resource. I do not know if you have heard of her adventures. She was told at Kokstad that she could not have a ticket for Pietermaritzburg unless she could produce a permit or Concession Form, so the resourceful little thing took a ticket for the station in the boundary between Natal and the Cape, and then took another ticket for Pietermaritzburg from there. Sometime when the office is not very busy, I will send you a copy of the letter. It fulfils my contention that although she cannot express herself in words, she can express herself in writing.

I hope we may have no trouble with her guardian. I suppose you must communicate with the Magistrate of Umtata about her, but if possible I should like her guardian not to know where she is.

If he gives trouble I am quite prepared to fight the issue even to the extent of appearing in Court if necessary. I have long felt that the powers of Native guardians for their women wards are excessive and often abused, and I would be prepared to expose the whole question if necessary.[2]

Please under no circumstances let her leave Adams without letting me know beforehand. I hope it may not come to this as I gather the guardian was mainly concerned that she should not cause him any expense, but of course he may be unwilling

---

1. Mr E.S. Bomback was the Bursar at Adams.
2. Clearly, Mabel's feminist sympathies were roused. Amongst her papers, is a set of notes on 'The legal difficulties of African women'.

to lose her services. Anyway, I am prepared to make a fight to give her an education if it is necessary.

After all I am enclosing a copy of the letter as I find the office is not so very busy.

Please tell Lily that I have written to you and that I will write to her in a day or two.

With kind regards to Mr Grant whom you will no doubt inform of this situation.

Yours very sincerely,
(Dr) Mabel Palmer

University of Natal, Durban
9th September, 1950

Mr Bomback,
Adams Mission.

Dear Mr Bomback,

Since the letter I wrote you yesterday with regard to Lily Moya, I have had an opportunity of discussing the situation with Mr Havemann, Manager of the Native Administration Department in Durban.[1]

His view is, that it would be unwise at this stage to bring the matter officially to the notice of the Magistrate since Lily is not only a Bantu girl, but a minor Bantu girl, and our legal position is extremely weak, and he thinks that if the matter were to come to any official action the girl would undoubtedly be called back.

He suggests that if possible, we should find some sympathetic person in Umtata who might be willing to enquire into the situation, and in particular to find out the attitude of the guardian. I do not know anybody in Umtata, but possibly Adams College may have say an old student in some position there, or some of the older members of the staff at Adams may know people at Umtata. If something can be done on these lines, Mr Havemann thinks it would be very much better than communicating with the Magistrate at this stage.

---

1. E.H. Havemann was the official in charge of the municipality's Native Administration Department.

He thinks that my willingness to fight on Lily's behalf would get us nowhere, and that a much more cautious approach is desirable. Perhaps you will let me know what Mr Grant thinks on the subject.

I asked Mr Havemann whether we should do anything or await action on the part of the guardian and Magistrate, but his view is that if I were alone concerned that is the course he would advise, but he feels some hesitation in suggesting this line of action to Adams College who might be unwilling to face any difficulties in the matter, in view of their official position.

Yours very sincerely,
(Dr) Mabel Palmer

Adams College, Natal
12/9/50

My dearest Dr Mabel Palmer,

Glad indeed to write you again. I suppose you understand that my first letter to you, here at Adams, was a little hurried off episode. I understand that you must be wondering what is the immediate cause of my turning up this end so suddenly before you'd sent me the concession as so on.

The climax if not reached, was about to be reached.[1] Besides all other reasons I once gave you before, all along our long correspondence I had never dared to tell you this but now I feel compelled to tell you that I could, or in fact try to endure every other difficulty patiently and humbly, but not to see myself getting married in an awkward manner, to a man I hated so much. That is one of the things I so much hate being married. I don't even dream about it. That awful bondage. That is what my uncle did to me. He wanted only the dowary.[2] Though

1. For the significance of this letter, see the Introduction, pp.21ff.
2. Strictly speaking, Africans in South Africa do not have a dowry system, which is normally a portion given with a bride to her husband. What Lily is referring to is *lobolo*, the bridewealth, usually in cattle, given by the husband's family to the family of the wife in exchange for her reproductive and labour power, and as security, should the marriage break up. Despite initial missionary strictures against *lobolo*, Christian Africans continued to pay it, but by this time it was being paid at least as much in cash as in cattle.

N.E.E.D.—7

it embitters me to tell you this, I feel and understand it my duty to do so. Wishing and hoping it would be buried only in your kind heart.

I find Adams a very nice place. Kindness around and near.

I don't know yet whether I'll have to sit for the Exams this term ending. In fact I should have been in Form V. I suppose I had been placed in Form IV only to have a better foundation for Form V next year. I hope to show my best in Form V next year.

These are the subjects I take.

1) English
2) Maths
3) Zulu B
4) Geography
5) Botany
6) Zoology
7) Agriculture

I shall write you a more pleasant letter next time.

With heartiest Greetings.

Yours affectionately,
Lily P. Moya

P.S. Will not be quite happy unless I hear from you.

Adams College, Natal
18.9.50

My dearest Dr Mabel Palmer,

I hardly know how to begin my letter as you haven't yet replied my two letters. I suppose the reason is that you are busy. I hope you are well and happy. ·

I was given the books on the 12th inst. on Friday (all, except those few out of stock).

I'm feeling homely,[1] although the difficulty is that I have to be borrowed blankets, sheet and uniform. I wouldn't care for second hands uniform.

---

1. i.e. at home.

I suppose you are really finding a difficult with me as I am solely on my own. Please do not get tired of me. Adopt me to the end as you have done.

I can just say I am happy here, I'm alright. I cann't help those who are very good at laughing at others. Perhaps they are not used to such individuals like me who have striven nearly all their lives under unsympathetic individuals and who have been brought up in poverty.[2] They will soon get used to me as soon as I get some of the articles and, am no borrower. I can be glad to complete next year my Form V here unless you decide some other place or plans for me. I mean, I am prepared to do as your will.

Can I come some Fridays to see you there in Durban? Mrs 'Bomburgh'[3] has promised to take me with her at any Friday it will be convenient for you to see me. She has also given me a jersey to put on a towel and a cake of soap. Had it not been for your kindness I wouldn't have seen the place and never have received such presents.

I can be very glad if you would reply my letters as I will have no privelege of writing you due to stamps and so on.

It makes me happy receiving a letter from you. Please do write. I know you are very busy. You are doing one of the greatest works.

Best wishes and love,
Yours very affectionately,
Lily P Moya

Handwritten note at the top of the letter of 18.9.50
Wrote Sept. 21 telling her £5 sent for her expenses and to have 10/— a month pocket money and will phone Bombacks next week about bringing her in. M. Palmer

---

2. An early sign of the teasing to which Lily was subjected.
3. Mrs Bomback, the wife of the Bursar.

Circular Letter from the Principal of Adams

Adams College, Natal
18.9.50

To Parents and Guardians:

A fortnight ago I informed you that there was some unrest at the College and that I had sent home those students who had failed to attend chapel. Since then, with the help of my three Head Teachers and the Dean, I have been trying to find out what the cause of the unrest was, and who were responsible for it. I can now give you an account of our findings.[1]

First of all, the trouble began, when in keeping with established school policy, I refused to make an exception and give permission to the Zulu Society to hold a dance in the Tshaka Day celebrations.[2] This refusal was resented, largely because the student Chairman wrongly and wilfully misinterpreted the ruling, contending that though dancing by itself was not permissible, dancing in a play was. Let me add that dancing at any school celebrations has not been allowed for at least three years, as it has tended to arouse inter-tribal conflict.[3]

Smarting under a sense of grievance at my refusal to allow dancing, the Chairman of the Zulu Society called an unauthorised meeting of the Zulus (males only)[4] on Wednesday evening, the 30th Aug., and sought ways and means of embarrassing the school authorities. In their discussions the words revenge and retaliation were used. It was here suggested that in order to win

1. See Introduction p.28 for the significance of these events.
2. The Zulu Society was founded in 1937 by members of the Zulu intelligentsia, to gain recognition for the Zulu monarchy and to restructure 'traditional life' which it was felt was disintegrating in the face of African urbanisation and proletarianization. The Tshaka or Shaka Day celebrations were established by Solomon kaDinuzulu, heir to the last Zulu king as part of a more widespread 'invention of tradition'. (See chapter 2 in Marks, *The Ambiguities of Dependence* for this revival.) Its celebration at Adams had been encouraged by Edgar Brookes. (See Brookes, *A South African Pilgrimage*, 64.) By the 1950s it had become a major event amongst Zulu nationalists. Shaka was the military founder of the Zulu kingdom and its dynasty.
3. For 'inter-tribal conflict' at Adams, see Introduction, p.28.
4. For the 'patriarchy' of the Zulu Society, see note 109, citing the Charter, and Marks, 'Patriotism, patriarchy and purity: Natal and the politics of Zulu ethnic consciousness', in L. Vail, *The Political Economy of Ethnicity in Southern Africa* (forthcoming).

the approval and support of the non-Zulu students, the grievance should take the form of a complaint against food.[5] So, on the following evening, Thursday, the 31st Aug., at a second un-authorised meeting it was decided not to sing in chapel on the morrow and not to eat food at lunch time. On Friday, the 1st Sept., they succeeded in carrying out both these designs. Nothing was wrong with the food that day, for the girls ate theirs. Furthermore, on the following day when similar food was served they ate it without murmur. In addition, a group of students succeeded in persuading or preventing most of the student body from attending afternoon classes.

Faced with such a threat to school discipline, I consulted the Chairman of our Governing Council and sought police protection for those students who did not join in the defiance of school authority, and to protect school property.

At 3.15 p.m. that afternoon, I spoke to the students and told them that if they did not return to their classes by 4.00 p.m. they would be sent home. The Inspector of Schools, who was present, also spoke to them. At 4.00 p.m. few had obeyed my orders, so I told the disobedient ones to pack up and go home. They paid no heed to my words and remained where they were.

At this point − for the first time − some of the students intimated that their grievance was the food. Though this seemed to be an excuse and not the reason for their disobedience, the Chairman of the Governing Council with Mr. Selby Ngcobo[6] and Mr. Rubenstein[7] approached the students, and succeeded in persuading them that the manner in which they had chosen to express their grievance was wrong. The outcome was that three of the number came to me that evening to apologise for the behaviour and to promise to take what punishment I deemed fitting.

The following day, Saturday the 2nd Sept., I spoke to the students, and among other things warned them that should they

5. Complaints over food were extremely common in African schools in South Africa in the first half of the century, and not infrequently sparked off disturbances. (See Frank Molteno, 'The historical foundations of the schooling of black South Africans', 79.)
6. For Selby Ngcobo, MP to LM, 14.4.1949, note 1.
7. Mr D.H. Rubenstein was the Vice Principal.

offend in a similar manner again I would not hesitate to send them home. Not long after I sent for four students whom I had good reason to believe were responsible for the trouble and sent them home. There were still others, however, who were bent on causing further trouble.

That very afternoon, under the guise of a football practice, a large number of students met, and this time by way of retaliation they proposed the following measures:

(a) The breaking into of the food store-room and destroying the food.

(b) 'Taking care' of the night watchman, the Head Prefect and the Head Waiter.

(c) The burning down of the Dining Hall.

(d) The cutting of the telephone wires.

Of these four, only the first two were approved of, the latter two were disapproved of, one on the grounds that it was 'going too far', the other on the grounds that it would be damaging Government property. The time fixed for the execution of these proposals was 12.30 a.m.

Aware that mischief was afoot, I set a guard that night. A few students ventured out shortly after midnight, but sensing that their movements were watched, they returned to their dormitories and called the expedition off.

Early next morning, however, some of these same students went about telling boys not to eat their porridge at breakfast and not to go to church. (The porridge did have lumps in it, but it was eaten by the girls and by members of the staff). So in accordance with instructions the boys did not eat their porridge; and worse still, they failed to assemble for church parade.

Once again I went to them, and reminding them of what I had said only the day before in accepting their apology, I told them that if they did not go to church I would send them home. I also assured them that if they had any complaints about the food they could send six of their number to see me after chapel. In spite of my warning only a small percentage of the students went to church. Many did not go 'for fear of being thrashed'.

In face of such repeated disobedience, I had no option but to send the disobedient students home. This I did with the full approval of my Head Teachers, and such members of the

Council as were able to be present. I was able to do this without any injury to person or property, as police protection was at hand.

Before the students left I told them that they could apply for re-admission but that they must be prepared to submit to an interview. At the same time Dr. Taylor of McCords Hospital[8] kindly offered to provide accommodation for any student who lived at a distance so that they might have their interview in Durban and thus avoid the expense of a journey home.

Further, to enable as many students as possible to have their interview with the least possible delay, the Head Teachers, the Dean, and I visited Durban on Tuesday and Wednesday (the 5th and 6th) and interviewed no less than 75 students at 86 Beatrice Street.[9] We made it clear to each one that we expected him to tell us what he thought the cause of the trouble was, and who were the ones responsible for it. If he would not answer our questions, we sent him to the end of the queue to think again; if, on the second occasion, he still refused to answer our questions we sent him home to think again. But it must be clearly understood — and this is to contradict false statements — that no student who came before us for an interview was sent home without first finding out whether he had a ticket and money to get home. If he made known his needs, he was provided with money to meet both the rail and bus fare and food expenses as well.

At the time of writing no less than 125 students have already been readmitted, while at least 50 more are about to be interviewed.[10]

No doubt you are asking many questions, and perhaps the uppermost one in your mind is this: 'was it necessary to send the students home? Could some other method of dealing with the situation not have been found?' The answer is 'no'. The evidence has borne out our judgement that a small gang was by intimidation causing students to defy school authority, and so getting in train a spirit of rank lawlessness. Had the members

8. See notes on 9.9.1949 and 29.9.1949.
9. The headquarters of the American Zulu Mission in Durban.
10. There were about 450 students at Adams altogether at that time, so that a very considerable proportion of the male students was involved.

111

of this gang been allowed to continue on the premises, then they would ere long have succeeded in wrecking the school. It was only by getting all disobedient students off the premises, and then interviewing them that we could learn who the mischief makers were. To our great disappointment many many of our students were either too frightened or too acquiescent to oppose the activities of the gang.

I am grateful to you for the many letters of sympathy and approval which you have sent me. If I have not answered them please understand that pressure of work has prevented me. I trust that ere long conditions at the College will be back to normal. I am aware that the course adopted has meant anxiety and loss to many of you, and acute hardship to not a few of the students. This I regret. Yet I saw no way else of dealing with a dangerous threat to College discipline — yes, a threat also to non-sympathetic students and to College property.

Finally, boys who went home will not be given permission to go home over the October holidays. The girls may go to their homes in and near Durban, but in view of recent happenings parents are advised not to ask for their children to be allowed to go to Durban unless they are actually going home.

Greetings to you all.

G.C. Grant,
Principal.

Holard Cottage
P.O. Adams College
24/9/50

My dearest Dr Mabel Palmer,

Thank you very much for your most sweet compassion towards me. I really thank you, though I cannot outwardly reveal my thanks.

God Bless you to the end. I hope and pray Him to thank you, for me, I must repeat this again. I have no means of thanking you. I find my verbal thanks too inferior to your kindness.

I can be glad if I can see you frequently. Your letter has been the source of inward happiness. I am really glad, glad indeed. O, it was a blessing. It has cleared me off the doubt the anxiety, the upsetness of mind. You know, when one is in diffucalty, also mentally becomes impressed I think I'll be like other individuals. I mean to devote myself divinely because a human being without religion is no better than a shade of herself.

I hope you stay for years, with me. You cannot leave me alone in this merciless world.

Love and greetings,

Yours affectionately,
Lily

With the money you sent for me Mr & Mrs Bomburgh[1] have bought me two blankets and a calico to make sheets and pillow cases. I think there will be two sheets from that material. Thanks ever so much for the will. Your love has tongue-tied me.

'Ditto'

University of Natal, Durban
26th. September, 1950

The Principal,
Adams College.

Dear Mr Grant,

Thank you very much for sending me your notice about your recent difficulties. I found it very interesting reading and was glad to know exactly what had occurred.

You must feel gratified that you escaped any damage to property, such as occurred on a similar occasion some years ago.[2]

I hope everything is settling down again comfortably.

With renewed thanks,

I am,
Yours sincerely,
(Dr) Mabel Palmer

1. Bomback.

2. The cases of unexplained arson in 1947 during which the dining hall burnt down.

My dearest Dr Mabel Palmer,

Glad indeed to have this noble chance of writing you this missive. The journey on the whole, back, was a safe one. By the time we reached Amanzimtoti it was fairly dark and I had a good-luck to arrive with some girls who had gone for shopping.

I wish to express my thanks for the hospital[1] reception you made me. I was really happy with you, and was a little heart-aching when you persuaded me to hurry off for the train. The good humoured old man was kind enough to take me to Berea Station, as the tram was a little bit late for the down station train. I wouldn't restrain myself from telling matron that I was very happy in Durban and didn't want to come back on Saturday.

I'm busy copying notes which were given from the beginning of last term. I have finished Agricultural notes and now am about to finish the Zoology.

We have eleven English set books. They have taken five and finished the other one Edwin Drood. I have finished reading on my own one of the set-books, a play by Shakespeare (The Twelfth Night). It is a little strain to rush for what people have done and far off in, but, it is all the better to speed on this month, so that next year I be on good standard with them.

I will not refuse to write the Exams but all the same I wish it is not forgotten that I ought to be in Form V, because I am a Form V failure and that I had been out of school for quite a long time.

I shall write and tell you how far I'm proceeding.

With greetings and love,

Yours affectionately,
Lily Moya

1. Hospitable

University of Natal, Durban
4th October, 1950

The Manager,
Native Administration Dept.,
Pietermaritzburg.

Dear Mr Bang,[1]

I am afraid I have been some time in thanking you for having arranged to have that native girl Lily Moya met and despatched on her way, to Durban.

At the time I rang you up I was a good deal in the dark about what was happening, but it now appears that the intrepid little creature, who had never been in a railway train before or used a telephone, had run away in order to escape from a distasteful marriage, and had never received the concession from Adams College, which I was assuming was in her possession.

She had quite a number of adventures, but did ultimately arrive at Adams, and is now comfortably installed there. I gather she was much relieved when the Railway police met her and helped her on her way.

With many thanks for your kindly co-operation,

I am,

Yours very truly,
(Dr) Mabel Palmer

University of Natal, Durban
6th October, 1950

Mr. Bomback,
Mary Lyons Hostel,
Adams College.

Dear Mr Bomback,

I was very much interested in seeing Lily Moya on Saturday, but she certainly took a risk in coming to see me without notice, as I might have been out. Fortunately, however, I was at home and was able to talk to her for a couple of hours. It

1. Mr D.N. Bang, a fluent Zulu linguist who later joined the Department of African Studies, University of Natal, Pietermaritzburg.

was definitely a case of 'talking to her' because her tongue-tied shyness in conversation is the most perfect contrast to her vigour and lack of self-consciousness when she has a pen in her hand.

I impressed on her that she must settle down at Adams and must not expect to see too much of me, but she said she very much wanted to see the sights of Durban.

I wonder if you ever have excursions for your students from a distance to show them Durban? If not, could you send Lily and say another couple of girls with her. I would arrange to find a guide for them and give them lunch at the International Club, but please let me have at least a week's notice. A week-day afternoon I think would be best as the girl I have in mind as a guide has classes on Saturday mornings.

Another point – Will you be sure that Lily enters for the form of Matriculation which admits to the Universities? Whether she will be good enough for University education is, of course, still uncertain, but I would like to be sure that she has left no obstacles behind her in her path.

I was very glad to learn that she was taking Mathematics as that is essential for the Medical Degree, and if she were very good and could manage to get Class I in Matriculation (which I do not suppose is very likely) she might apply for one of the quite generous scholarships which the Government is putting at the disposal of Bantu students, i.e. £150 for the first two years and £200 for the five following years.[1]

Lily said something about a telegram which she said had been received from me. I never sent you a telegram. If I have to communicate with Adams I much prefer to do it by 'phone. Probably she was making a mistake.

Please be very sure if any difficulty arises not to let Lily go without letting me know first. She tells me that she is running

1. As previously noted, Mabel was heavily involved with the opening of the Durban Medical School in 1951. In that year, the government made available fifteen scholarships for black students. One went to a black woman; most went to Indians. The number was pitiful, given the number of African doctors at the time: until World War II, when the University of Witwatersrand and then Cape Town opened their doors to black medical students, Africans had to study medicine abroad. There were no more than thirty African doctors in South Africa in 1950 (*The Star*, 13.1.1950).

away from a distasteful marriage into which her guardian was forcing her, and I feel that she should be protected from that. However, as you have heard nothing, I hope that you will perhaps still hear nothing and that the Magistrate has decided to take no steps in the situation.

Have you seen Negley Farson's 'Last Chance in Africa'?[2] There are some very curious and not very accurate references to the career of one of our former students, yours and ours — David Warohio on Page 209 following.[3]

The References to the University of Natal are so inaccurate that I am suggesting to the Principal that he should write to the author on the subject.

It appears, however, that Warohio is now doing very well in Kenya.

With many thanks for the co-operation of Mrs Bomback and yourself in looking after Lily,

I am,
Yours sincerely,
(Dr) Mabel Palmer

2. Negley Farson (born Plainfields, New Jersey, 1890, died 1960) was a well-known journalist, who wrote several books on Africa. *Behind God's Back*, his autobiography, published in 1940, became a bestseller and was republished in 1983 by Hamlyn paperbacks (Aylesbury, Bucks) with a tribute by Colin Wilson. *Last Chance in Africa* based on trips made to Kenya in 1939 and 1947 was published in London and Southampton in 1947.
3. According to Farson, David Waruhiu, son of one of the most prominent Kikuyu chiefs, had been educated by American missionaries, at the Alliance High School in Kenya, King's College, Uganda, Adams and then at the University of Natal. Farson's account of Waruhiu's sojourn in Natal is somewhat colourful, but it is not clear what Mabel found inaccurate either here or in his account of the University. Farson describes Chief Waruhiu, David Waruhiu's father, as 'about the only man I met in Africa in whom I felt the teaching of Christianity had completely fulfilled its mission' (p. 209ff). It was Chief Waruhiu's death in 1952 which sparked off the 'Mau Mau' emergency. (I am grateful to Dr John Lonsdale for additional information on the Waruhiu family.)

117

Dr Mabel Palmer,
P.O. Box 1525, Durban.

Dear Dr Palmer,

Lily Moya

Please forgive me for not having replied to your letters before — I had hoped to have some news from the Magistrate of Umtata. He does not, apparently, consider the matter at all urgent as we are still awaiting his reply.

I enclose our receipt for the £5 you sent for Lily's bedding. This was purchased from the wholesaler and cost as follows:

5 yards of 62″ sheeting 7/9 per yard	£1.18.9.
2 woollen blankets 25/6 each	2.11.0.
Advance for travelling to Durban on 30.9.50	7.6.
	£4.17.3.

My wife tells me that Lily requires a gym tunic and white blouse, and I presume it will be in order for us to purchase it on your behalf.

Yours sincerely,
S. Bomback
Bursar

University of Natal, Durban
13th October, 1950

Mr E.S. Bomback,
Adams College.

Dear Mr Bomback,

I have your letter of the 9/10/50 with regard to Lily Moya. Please arrange for her to have the Gym Tunic, and anything else within reason that she may need.

I will send you some more money if you need it and notify me of the amount required.

Yours sincerely,
(Dr) Mabel Palmer

My dearest Dr Mabel Palmer,

I am really glad to write you this letter. I wish to tell you that do not be disappointed with me if I do not finish reading the book you gave me before the holidays. I am very busy copying notes and trying to collect some few points in set books. Had I enough time I would gladly read it, knowing that it must have some good teaching to me either literally or in behaviour of good conduct or, in both ways beneficial to me.

I'm not going to worry you too much either with too many letters but you talked to me about something, making friends with other girls.

It is a very difficult case, because a friend must be somebody one understands well or other somebody who must understand one well. It is difficult to a person like myself especially who has just come.

Time is too little for me to talk with others not that I'm thinking highly of myself but that they're too high for me have their own friends already and have their own affairs to discuss. It is quite difficult to intrude myself into others secrets.

I admit that my association is a very dull one to other girls. I have no attractions at all to anybody.

Sometimes I feel circumstances enforcing me to stealing myself away from their associations which ninety-nine out of a hundred is always ended in a sort of quarel or some sort of defermation[1] of character.

You see, there has been a certain girl who called herself a friend to me. She braided my hair, and invited me for a jive which things are as I investigated somehow all out of school rules.

Don't you think friends sometimes mislead or say they always mislead because I haven't been lucky myself in having what is called a real friend, though I would like to have one if it would be a good one to understand me.

How must I choose a good, real friend, and by whose friendship I can gain not only socially but also spiritually.

One of the weaknesses I have is that I'm very bad at having

---

1. i.e. defamation.

a friend, not like others who easily make friends and acquaintaintances wherever they go.

I prefer walking alone in fact I am bound to. For instance, I opened my heart to the other girl and told her of my troubles, how I had been tyrannical held down by the strong hands and how I had been stinted of education, liberty, money, dress, the necessaries of life and the commonest pleasures of childhood which have so much affected my outlook to my watchers and so on, and has caused me to be unable to express my myself properly so that I can be well understood by others, instead of being friendly to me she became the opponent who flourished the news to others to make a bad impression of myself to everybody and to cause them to look down at me. I wonder how can I manage to get a friend.

By trying to attatch myself with the authorities, I mean visiting them frequently and being seen talking with them almost frequently, I am looked upon as being someone thinking highly of herself and who somewhat is a spy on others.[2]

Advise me. Do not get tired telling what you would like me to be, like I mean the ideal of myself, and of listening to some of my unlimited grievances.

Don't you think I should do away with friends as long as they do not satisfy me spiritually and as a good carieer of a school girl.

I don't mean I am extra-ordinary religious or so on. There are some girls who are quite good but it is very difficult intruding myself in their company and asking them to be my friend.

You shall not be disappointed, please do not, if I never write you a letter telling you of a friend.

You shall excuse me for this bad hand writing and untidiness of your letter. This pen is very bad. My fountain pen just vanished all of a sudden. No one seems to be knowing where it went.

Let me stop for today. I shall write you next time after you have replied me.

My greetings and love,

Yours very sincerely,
Lily Moya

2. This accusation may well have related to the tense atmosphere at Adams at the time of Lily's arrival. See Introduction, p.28.

P.S. You talked of 'international party visit'.[3] When do you think it suitable for me to come? Though I am very busy I can be glad to hear from you when to come.

University of Natal, Durban
4th November, 1950

Miss S Makhanya,
P.O. Umbumbula

Dear Miss Makhanya,

I wonder if it would be possible for you to take some interest in a little protege of mine? She is Lily Moya, and she is now a pupil at Adams College. (I am paying for her.)

She got into touch with me some years ago and told me she was an orphan, very anxious for education and that her Guardian would not consent to sending her away to school. Her letters were so lively and well written that I became quite interested in her, sent her books and tried to raise a small fund from the University women in Durban for her education. In this, however, I was unsuccessful and I finally decided just to undertake the charge myself.

Finally Lily was faced with the threat of being married to a much older man whom she disliked and without awaiting for arrangements to be completed for her to attend Adams College, she ran away; she got to Kokstad, the intrepid little thing, had never been in a train or used a telephone before but she phoned me. Naturally I could make very little of what she said, but I did just gather that she was arriving in Pietermaritzburg and wanted me to meet her there, which of course was quite impossible. However, I arranged with Mr Bang, who is the head of the Municipal Affairs in Pietermaritzburg, to have her met by the Railway Police on her way to Amanzimtoti, where she finally arrived and was enrolled in the School.

Lily does not seem to be settling down very satisfactorily, of course it is difficult for a girl coming in the middle of a term

3. There is a note here in Mabel's hand, 'Reference is to International Club where the party could have a rest and lunch'.

N.E.E.D.—8

like that, and she is I am afraid a very self centred young person.

I went down to Adams to see her and she came up and spent an afternoon with me in Durban, but it is a little difficult for me to do much for her. I think it would be unwise to have her as an overnight guest, as I so pleasantly had you some years ago, because she is already, I think, a little puffed up by my interest in her and being so self centred she is a little inclined to presume on it. I feel she could be more effectively helped by a woman of her own race, and I would be extremely grateful if you could see her and perhaps invite her to your Settlement.[1] I would gladly pay any charges necessary for her and would be very glad indeed if you could help her to learn to think more of other people and less of herself.

I think she is very well worth helping, she certainly can write. Her letters are most interesting and amusing although mainly about herself. I have in mind that she might be encouraged to be a journalist, but of course at first that could not be her main source of livelihood, but she could do a teacher's course and write in her spare time.[2] She certainly has character and initiative. When she tried to take a ticket to Pietermaritzburg for Kokstad, they refused to give her one as she had no permit of any kind, so she took a ticket to the Border instead, nipped out of the carriage and took a ticket to Pietermaritzburg, dreading all the time that she might be discovered and sent back to her Location[3] near Umtata. She will be a very unhappy woman though unless she can be helped out of her present self absorption.

It would be very kind of you if you could give me a little aid in this direction.

Venturing to thank you in anticipation.

I am,
Yours sincerely,
Mabel Palmer

1. The Social Centre at Umbumbulu; the model in Mabel's mind was perhaps a 'Settlement' like Toynbee Hall in the East End of London established in the 1880s by Christian missionaries and students to carry out 'social work' amongst the City's poor.
2. Mabel was constantly planning Lily's future career. See, for example, below, MP to LM, 12.1.51 and 21.6.51.
3. Reserve.

P.S. I wish you would let me know sometime when you are going to be in Durban so that we can meet again. I am unfortunately much crippled by arthritis and find it extremely difficult to get about now a days.

Mabel Palmer

Adams College.
13 November, 1950

Dr Mabel Palmer,
P.O. Box 1525, Durban.

IMPORTANT

Dear Madam,

Lily Moya

I write to remind you that the following payments for your ward are still due:

School Fees	£7.10.0.
Doctor's Fees	– – –
Examination Fees	– – –
Domestic Science	– – –
Advance	–
Total	£7.10.0.

Unless I hear from you by return of post I shall reluctantly be compelled to prevent her from sitting her examinations which begin on the 20th of this month.

I expect an immediate reply; so you are urged to attend to this matter without delay.

Yours faithfully,
G.C. Grant
Principal

Miss Lily Moya,
C/o Adams College.

Dear Miss Moya,

I have just time for a word and will write you a longer letter in my own writing later on about the question of making friends etc.

I am sorry that it is quite impossible for me to see you on Friday next, 17th inst. I am always at the office on that day and very busy. Friday is the busiest day for me. Also I rang up Mr Bomback this morning and he tells me that he is not coming in on Friday. He tells me that he will bring you in a little later on and will let me know when he is coming.

I asked Adams College to make you a pocket money allowance of 10/- a month, to be charged to me, but perhaps they may not have understood, and are thinking that I send it to you. Will you let me know whether or not you receive this 10/- a month?

I have no time for more at present but Mr Bomback tells me that you safely received the fountain pen, and I hope you will find it useful.

I have written about you to a Mrs Makanya of the Umbululu Settlement,[1] and I understand from Mr Bomback that she is hoping to get into touch with you. She is a most remarkable person and I am sure that you will enjoy any contact with her that she may be able to arrange.

With all good wishes,

> I am,
> Yours very sincerely,
> (Dr) Mabel Palmer

---

1. Miss Makhanya (Sibusisiwe Makhanya never married), of the Umbumbulu Social Centre. Mabel treats Sibusisiwe Makhanya's name and address with singular lack of concern for precision throughout the correspondence.

Dear Mr Bomback,

I enclose herewith a cheque for £7.10.0. for Lily Moya's fees. I wonder if you could be kind enough to send me a note of what her fees will be for next year, and a rough estimate of incidental clothes, etc. including the charge for her residence in holidays. Would you rather I sent her 10/- a month for pocket money? I will if you would prefer it, but it is rather a burden to get a postal order and I rather hoped you would give it to her and received from me later.

I hope I may get some sort of report on her progress. With thanks for the cooperation of yourself and Mrs Bomback in looking after the poor little thing.

I am,
Yours very sincerely,
Mabel Palmer

Adams College
20.11.50

Dr Mabel Palmer,
24 Clair Avenue, Durban.

Dear Dr Palmer,

Thank you for your letter of the 16th November in which you enclosed a cheque for £7.10.0. for Lily Moya's fees. I enclose a receipt for this.

I enclose a copy of our prospectus, which gives details of the fees payable.

At the end of the term I shall send you a full account of all the expenditure on behalf of Lily.

We shall arrange to send Lily's school report to you.

Yours faithfully,
E.S. Bomback
Bursar

ADAMS HIGH SCHOOL

Report to parent on   *LILY MOYA*   Date   *4/12/50*

Parent or Guardian   *Dr. MABEL PALMER*   Form   *IV*
                        Natal University
                        College, Durban

	MARKS			
SUBJECT	Obtained	Maximum	Minimum	REMARKS
ENGLISH	*180*	*400*	*104*	*Fair. Shows promise*
GEOGRAPHY	*130*	*350*	*117*	
VERNACULAR B	*150*	*300*	*100*	*Fair.*
LATIN, AFRIKAANS				
BOTANY	*175*	*350*	*117*	*Good. Hard worker*
ZOOLOGY	*179*	*350*	*117*	*Very fair*
AGRIC' SCIENCE	*156*	*350*	*117*	*Good*
MATHEMATICS	*134*	*400*	*134*	
BIOLOGY				
TOTALS	*1104*			

No. in class   *22*   Class position   *13*

CONDUCT: *Satisfactory*

Passed Class II. Has worked well. Somewhat nervous but possibly this due to the fact that she had so much to do in rather a short period — otherwise satisfactory. Read up your English set books during holidays.

                 B.M. MTSHALI   HEAD TEACHER

School reopens   *7/2/51.*   Fees owing

N.B. No student will be re-admitted next term unless all accounts are paid up.

                 A satisfactory beginning

                     C. GRANT   PRINCIPAL

My dearest Dr Palmer,

It is of greatest pleasure to have this leisure of writing you. All along I had been wishing to write to and to hear from you. Exams sustained me and lately the worrying about of accommodation during the Holidays. I was released when I heard from Mrs Bomback that you had asked them to arrange for me for the Holidays. I am now here in Mary Leon Mr & Mrs Bomback's place. I am really grateful to them for taking me and to you for asking them.

I have never seen nor heard anything from Miss Makhala of Umbubulo.[1]

I hoped to be nearer you during the Holidays so that I should see you frequently as I really miss you and worried by your silence.

Kindly ask Mr & Mrs Bomback to take me along with them to town to see you. Please do not forget.

You have not written me that promised letter of how to make friends. Your silence really makes me nervous.

I hoped and thought silently that I would be of greatest help to you during the Holidays, since it is your will that I should stay here in Adams and, besides; Mrs Bomback always helps me when I'm in trouble, I'm quite satisfied.

Cann't I try writing articles chosen by you next year for publication? How have I carried on these three months in school work. I'm anxious to know. If you don't mind tell me. I had been told some of the marks I scored in few subjects.

I hope you are well and happy. Please don't overwork yourself, have a mental as well as a physical rest.

Every morning when I wake up and every evening before going to bed, I remember you in my prayers and even when I'm walking alone. You have made me a someone in the world, and released me spiritually. You have alleviated my burden.

1. Miss Makhanya of Umbumbulu.

O! Goodbye! Happiest Life, happiest Christmast and Long live!

Yours very sincerely,
Lily

P.S. I hope you will not get tired of advising me and of writing me.   'The Same'

University of Natal, Durban
15th December, 1950

Mr Bomback,
Mary Lyon Hostel,
P.O. Adams Mission

Dear Mr Bomback,

I was very glad to have your letter and to learn that you have been able to make some arrangements for Lily.

I am afraid I am giving you a good deal of trouble about her.

I wonder if you and Mrs Bomback could bring her in to spend the day with me sometime fairly soon, and perhaps I could give you tea and we could have a little talk about Lily in general.

I have been wondering whether I could have her with me for a week to help me in dusting my books, but I am not quite sure about it because I understand Mrs Bomback thinks that she is already inclined to think too much of herself, and if I had her to stay with me, it might intensify that tendency, so that I do not want to ask her to come and stay with me until I am sure that Mrs Bomback approves.

I enclose a letter for Lily which perhaps Mrs Bomback might like to read before she gives it to her.

I have myself been trying to find a respectable Bantu family with whom she might stay for a week or two in Durban. In that case she could come up to me to help with the dusting of the books every day. I am not sure, however, that I shall be successful. The Ngcobo's would have done it but unfortunately they are going to be away and their house shut up for the whole of the holidays.

Lastly, I hope you will not mind if I do not send you the cheque for £9 until sometime in January. I am at the present moment rather hard up, but I expect a big cheque for half yearly dividends in the middle of January. I had intended to realise a small amount of capital in order to pay for Lily but if I can manage to do it out of income, I would rather do that.[1]

I expect to be at home most days in the immediate future but not next Tuesday, and I suggest that in any case, it might perhaps be better if you were to 'phone me 888415, if you fall in with this suggestion at the beginning of this letter.

With many thanks for all the care you have taken of Lily.

I am,

Yours very sincerely,

(Dr) Mabel Palmer

University of Natal, Durban
15th December, 1950

Dear Lily,

I have written to Mr Bomback suggesting that he should bring you in to see me, and I have not forgotten you.

As a matter of fact I have been considering various plans for you, but none of them have yet come to a head.

I cannot borrow the book I want to send you anywhere in Durban, and the Librarian has sent for it from the State Library in Pretoria. I want to read it myself before I hand it on to you.

I enclose a Postal Order for 10/- in order to give you a little spending money over Christmas.

Hoping I may see you before long,

I am,

Yours sincerely,

(Dr) Mabel Palmer

1. The sums Mabel was disbursing for Lily were really very generous in view of her own straitened circumstances.

Mrs Bomback,
Mary Lyon Hostel,
P.O. Adams Mission

Dear Mrs Bomback,

This is to introduce to you Mr. S.N. MLALA, who is one of our students[1] and has a teaching post near Umbumbulu.

He has undertaken to see if he can show any kindness to Lily Moya.

Yours sincerely,
(Dr) Mabel Palmer

EDWARD S. BOMBACK
Mary Lyon Hostel, Adams College
[1/1/51][2]

My dearest Dr Palmer,

Greetings and Merry New Year!!!

Forgive me for writing you on this paper. Ever so many thanks for the lovely Xmas present you sent me. The view within it is a lovely one and has inspired me with hopes of visiting the places. Your typed name on the card has made me feel proud of it.

The journey back was a safe one. On Friday I went to Umbumbulu to visit Mr & Mrs Mlala. They are good people, but I'm quite happy here too with Mrs Bomback and she doesn't mind having me with her here. I thanked them for their kindness and as they asked me to come again at any time, I promised them to do so. I haven't heard anything from the Makhanyas.

I shall write you a longer letter next time.

With best wishes for your New Year,

Yours very sincerely,
Lily Moya

1. In the Non-European Section of the University of Natal.

2. This reads 1/1/1950 in the original — but is an obvious error for 1/1/1951.

My dearest Dr Mabel Palmer,

I have given Mr Bomback the list of articles I wish to have, some of them are compulsory as they are uniform. He said it is unlikely to get them as you haven't finished paying out, even last term's fee.

For quite a long time I had been thinking over this terrific[1] position of mine, understanding too the difficulty of helping someone totally helpless like myself, Don't you think that, (this is my decision at this moment), it would be better for me to finish up my Matriculation Course there in Durban this year. I understand there has been a decent family you had been asking me to stay with or else pay for my boarding and lodging at a much more reduced price in the Native Women's Municipal Hostel corner Grey Street and Dartnell Crescent (Telephone 21821) monthly fee is 5/- meals obtainable. I don't know whether this fee for the second place is correct. To my mind, it seems as if this would alleviate your burden and of course you know the best schools there in Durban which I can attend, although I don't know their fees, but, I hope it would be at a reduced price, too.

Then, in Durban I'll get in touch with your school, your people and with many other civilized branches[2] which would be of better use in my future because I admit and understand that my life entirely depends upon my education because, I know that no one will work for me, you have already strained yourself too much for me.

That is how I have solved this problem, but it is not a suggestion. It is too bitter to be a centre of attraction in a notorious manner.[3]

You can say to the College that you take me because you wish me to be nearer you and to get in touch with your University syllabus.

1. Terrible.
2. Aspects of civilization.
3. This hints again at Lily's incapacity to find friends at Adams, and her feeling of isolation at this time.

Kindly reply me at your earliest possible.
With Greetings,
    Best wishes for your New Year,
                            Yours very sincerely,
                            Lily Moya

                                        Adams College
                                        3.1.51

Dr Mabel Palmer,
P.O. Box 1525, Durban.

Dear Dr Palmer,

Lily has given me the enclosed list of requirements, telling me that you have agreed to her having them. A rough estimate shows that they will cost about £16, and at the moment none of them is essential. Bearing in mind that you have already requested that only necessary things should be purchased for her, I should like you to confirm that she is to have these articles.

Lily appears to be quite happy on her own, but it is a great pity that she would not stay for a few weeks with the Mtalas at Umbumbulu.[1]

                            Yours sincerely,
                            E.S. Bomback
                            Bursar

P.S. May I take this opportunity of wishing you an agreeable and satisfactory new year.   ESB.

List attached to the preceding letter
I am asking for these articles:

Uniform
            a Gymn dress
            Green blazer
            White Sunday dress
            2 pair of white Sunday shoes
            Green jersey

1. Mtala is presumably a mistake for Mlala. The episode remains obscure.

Schooling shoes
Underwears
Night dress, and,
Bed spread

I'm sorry I've toothache I would be giving you the least[1] myself.

Lily Moya

University of Natal, Durban.
12th January, 1951

Miss Lily Moya,
c/o Adams College.

Dear Lily,[2]

I have to answer two communications either from you or about you, and refer also the conversation between myself and Mrs Bomback on Wednesday afternoon.

I was very sorry to hear from Mrs Bomback that you had been breaking the College rules and also disobeying Mrs Bomback's express injunction when you entered the men Lecturer's hostel with the purpose of receiving a lesson from one of them. You must keep the College rules.[3] You must not display any spirit of insubordination towards Adams College.

I was further grieved to learn that you refused the offer of employment during the Vacation. I certainly think, you should have referred the matter to me (and you should refer similar offers in future). If Mr Dhlamini was willing to give you work in his house, you certainly ought to have taken it.[4] It would have relieved me of the payment of several pounds for your keep during the vacation, and it would also have been good for

---

1. The list.

2. This letter is perhaps one of the most significant in the sequence. See Introduction, pp.29–30.
3. The reason for the College rules is clear, but it would appear that Lily was acting in all innocence.
4. Given Lily's experiences of domestic work in Umtata, it was perhaps hardly surprising that she refused this offer. Dhlamini is a pseudonym for a teacher at Adams; see Lily's bitter attack on him, 8.6.51.

you even for a short time, to have been a part of an educated Bantu family.

And finally, I was sorry to hear that you would not accept Mr Mlala's invitation to stay a few days with them. I had gone to a good deal of trouble to see Mr Mlala, to explain the situation to him, and to ask him to arrange for you to have a little holiday up at Umbumbulu. Mr Mlala is one of our students and is an exceptionally nice and interesting person, and I am very much afraid you were not quite straight about this matter, because you certainly left me with the impression that Mrs Bomback did not approve of you accepting this invitation and that that was why you had refused it. Mrs Bomback, on the contrary, tells me that she urged you to accept it, even going so far as to say it was your duty to accept it.[5]

If you want to please and help me you will let nothing of this sort happen again. You should take every opportunity of making friends in educated families, and you should certainly earn any money that you can in the vacation in order at least to relieve me of the burden of providing for you in them.

As far as the list of things which you sent me and which you say is required is concerned, I think there was a certain amount of misrepresentation. Mrs Bomback says that you told her that I had agreed to you having them. That I certainly never did, and now that I have discussed the matter with Mrs Bomback, I do not feel that it is necessary that you should have any of them. Mrs Bomback tells me that you already have a Gym Dress and underclothing and Jumper, and that although there has been talk of making certain items compulsory, this has not yet been done. However, Mrs Dick[6] the lady who you saw with me when you visited me last, most kindly offered to make you a white dress after you had gone, so that if you will send me the necessary measurements, I will ask Mrs Dick to fulfil her very kind promise. I want you to have everything which a poor class of girl at Adams has. I do not want you to be different in any way from the others, but I am not prepared to pay for dressing

5. It is difficult to know how much these allegations were the result of genuine miscommunication, how much the result of Lily's attempts to manipulate the situation to her advantage.
6. A friend of Mabel's.

you on a height equivalent to that of the wealthiest girls in Adams.

As for your letter of the 2nd January 195[1], I had already considered much earlier the possibility of sending you to the womens' hostel, but I was informed that it was not a place suitable for young girls, in fact one of our Bantu staff members came to see me especially about it, warning me that it would be most unwise to send you there. We do not like even our women students to stay there, and they are much older than you, if it can be prevented.[7] I went to a great deal of trouble last year to secure other accommodation for two of our women students. In any case I think you are too young yet to be in Durban on your own. Even if I could find a satisfactory place for you to live in you would not find it easy to study and it would be a perpetual anxiety to me.

I think you must be mistaken in thinking that you are 'the centre of attraction in a notorious manner'. I am sure that the other students at Adams have something better to think of than yourself. In any case when the school re-opens you will be one of the old girls and it is the new girls who will be centre of attraction.

You will be much more likely to pass your matriculation examination if you stay at Adams and make yourself contented and work steadily, and I very strongly wish you to do so. It is true the expense is rather heavy on me but I think it is worth it.

And now I must say some things to you that you won't like, but I think it is right that the situation should be made perfectly plain to you. In the first place I have undertaken to pay your expenses at Adams until the end of 1951, but I have not undertaken to do anything more than that. After 1951 you must try and find work or earn some scholarship. If you did very well and got a first class in your matriculation (which I do not in the least expect) you might be eligible for a scholarship in the Medical School. Your difficulties would then be at an end, but I regard this as most unlikely. If you passed the matriculation second or third class, I understand that you could probably get a teaching post, although if you went in for

7. See MP to LM, 14.4.49 and MP to NC, Umtata, 14.4.49.

teaching as a permanent occupation you would have to take some extra training in educational methods. We would have to enquire as to how that would be possible when the time comes. You might also possibly qualify as a Health Assistant in one of the new Health Centres.[8] That too I will enquire about nearer the time.

If for any reason you do not pass your matriculation, then you must resign yourself either to becoming a nurse or going into domestic service, and as I said when you came to see me, do not despise domestic service. Any sort of work well and conscientiously done is well worth undertaking.

I want you to write to me and say that you understand these conditions and are prepared to adhere to them.

And now for more personal matters, which it is even more difficult to speak about, but which I also feel must be made plain.

You say that one of your reasons for wishing to be in Durban is that you want to see more of me, but have you ever asked yourself whether I wish to see more of you? As a matter of fact I do not. Your romantic and self-centred imagination has built up for you a picture in which you are to be my devoted and intimate friend. Now you must forgive me for saying that this is all nonsense. Even if you were a European girl of your age it would still be nonsense. What basis of companionship could there be between a quarter educated girl of eighteen and an experienced old lady like myself? And of course the racial situation in Durban makes all these things more difficult.

You must obviously make your friends among your own people, and I am sorry to hear from Mrs Bomback that you seem to have some objection to doing this.[9] If you have any

8. Following the recommendations of the 1942–4 National Health Services Commission, the Union government established some fifty health centres, based on Sidney and Emily Kark's pioneering venture at Polela. They were intended to provide promotive and preventive health care, and the Institute of Family and Community Health, Clairwood, Durban was established to train health assistants and other primary health workers for the health centres. Mabel would have known about the Clairwood Institute through her connections with the Medical School.
9. Despite Mabel's 'liberalism' this and much of the above reveals her racially stereotyped thinking: black people should automatically find their friends amongst other black people, whatever their cultural or class differences.

such objection I should advise you to get rid of it as soon as possible.

You say you want to help me. The best way that you can help me is by staying at Adams and doing as well as you can both in your work and getting on with the other students, and that would be the best return you can make for the kindness I am showing you. That kindness does not necessarily involve any personal or intimate friendship. Indeed such an intimate friendship is impossible and could only be achieved on the basis of equal interest and experience which does not exist between you and me.

Mrs Bernard Shaw, long ago, gave me a scholarship which she paid out of her own pocket in order that I might go and study in America. I did not for that reason expect to become her intimate friend. I wrote her a letter of thanks and then waited for her to make the next move. When she made no move whatever and I did not meet her personally at all until very much later, I did not feel that I had any grievance. The way in which you must pay me back is the way in which I am paying back Mrs Bernard Shaw, namely by extending help to another poor and ambitious student many years later when in a position to do so.

At all events you only bother me by these demands for a close and intimate friendship. Do not write to me as 'my dearest Doctor Mabel Palmer'. 'Dear Dr Palmer' is enough, and do not write to me more than once a month. You should also wait until I ask you to come and see me. Do not throw out hints or ask to come and see me. Do you not think that you are a little familiar and presuming? I am a very busy woman. A visit from you means that I have to give up practically ., whole day to you, and I cannot afford the time very often.

Mrs Bomback tells me that you are not supposed to have a day off from Adams more than once in a term on a Saturday. But as Saturday is not convenient to me she will see that you have some other day.

I am beginning to feel that you are a very self-centred and indeed selfish young woman, who thinks so perpetually of herself and what she wants that she has no thoughts to spare for other people. If you continue in this line you will only lay up for yourself inevitable disappointment. And further you will never be a writer. Looking back over my correspondence with you I realise that you only write interestingly and amusingly when you are writing about yourself. When I asked you to describe to me the life of a girl in a native reserve, your article was not very satisfactory. You have an extraordinary command of language for your age (although it entirely deserts you in conversation and that is one reason why you are a dull companion). I believe that you might do very useful work in the future. So far as I know there are no Bantu women who have been able to write about the life of their people and the difficulties of contact with the white civilisation. If you could do that you would be fulfilling a most important function in the development of your people, but you will only be able to do that if you can cease to think only of yourself and be genuinely interested in other people. You should steadily practise putting yourself in the position of the other person and trying to see things from their point of view.

As for friendship, friendship is a gift. It can never be achieved by force or cunning. You should begin by joining any group that you can and doing what you can to help the group without putting yourself forward or obtruding your own personality. If you do that you will find that people will begin to like you, and then it may be that you will find somebody who will be to you a real friend, but you should always think more what you can do for a friend than what she can do for you. As I said, you do what I myself have often done. I have felt that I wanted a friend; somebody has come along that seems to be suitable, and then after all he or she turns out to be quite different from what I imagined. That was not her fault, it was mine.[10] I never promised to do more than help you to get an education and if you are disappointed in not getting more from me, that is your fault.

I arranged with Mr Bomback that I would send you 10/- a month for pocket money, and I enclose 10/- in this letter, but I would like you to keep an account of how you spend it and let me have that account by the end of every month, and on receipt of it I will send you the next 10/-.

10. A hint perhaps at Mabel's own personal loneliness, which she overcame through 'a busy and useful life': see Introduction, p.3.

Now I can imagine that this letter will probably be a shock to you, and I am also convinced that it will be a salutary shock and is written with your best interests in mind.

Pull yourself together; stop thinking that you can have everything you want; do not turn into a self-centred little snob or I shall have cause to regret that I offered you the help that rescued you from your natural position in life.

Yours sincerely,
(Dr) Mabel Palmer

Sending copy to Bombacks. Will arrange days sightseeing and lunch at Int. Club when I can find suitable Bantu girl as guide — But not early.

Mary Lyon Hostel, Adams College
16/1/51

Dear Dr Palmer,

Your letter has extremely shocked me. I'm very very sorry to give you such an evil impression of myself — to be ungrateful and unwilling to do work. I'm willing to work during vacations. It would be totally stupid of me to defy work after I have benefited so much from it.

Forgive and forget. I shall do my level best to show you the best of myself. I will not worry you at all, neither will I trouble Mrs Bomback.

I hope time will tell the reality of me.

Many thanks for the 10/- and hearty thanks too to Mrs Dick for her kindness. I shall try to do all you have told me to do. Please do forgive me, please.

One of the staff members is helping me with some work, since Tuesday last week, (9th inst.) Mrs Mac Niellage, and she and Mr Mac Niellage[1] are paying me daily. I shall tell you later how I've spent the money I'm earning. They are very kind people indeed.

I'm really ashamed of myself. I wish you forget my ungratefullness. Really I've misinterpreted myself with my actions.

---

1. Mr G.H. McNiellage was the head of the Industrial School at Adams.

There is a note for Mrs Dick, please, read it at first, before handing it to her.

Greetings.

I am,

Yours sincerely,

Lily

P.S. If you think the letter is unnecessary for Mrs Dick, you needn't give her but tear it and tell her the measurements. I'm really afraid to make another thing to annoy you or anybody else.

'Same'

24 Clair Avenue, Durban
18 Jan. 1951

Dear Lily,

I was very glad to have your letter and to find you had taken mine as it was meant. I was really sorry to seem so harsh, but you had got on a wrong track, and something was needed to bring you over on to the right track.

But I think so far you have succeeded in getting on to the right track. Both your letter to me and that to Mrs Dick were all they ought to be.

Are you going to send me any trial articles to criticise? Or are you going to be too busy with your studies for Matric?

All wishes for a Happy New Year.

Yours v. sincerely,
Mabel Palmer

University of Natal, Durban
20th January, 1951

Miss S. Makhanya,
P.O. Umbumbulu.

Dear Miss Makhanya,

I have never had any answer from you about Lily Moya, although Mrs MacDonald[1] told me that when she saw you with

---

1. This was Mrs Florence MacDonald, a close friend of Mabel Palmer's

Sibusisiwe Makhanya with a class at Umbumbulu.

Sibusisiwe's house at Umbumbulu.

Tea interval: Mabel Palmer and Florence MacDonald at the Winter School at Adams, *c.* 1939.

Adams College:

> *Above:* Dining hall
> *Right:* Mrs E. S. Bomback
> *Below:* Mary Lyon House

Foundation stone ceremony, Lyman K. Seymour High School, August 1949.
(L to R) The Hon. Mr D. G. Shepstone, Administrator of Natal,
Mr Jack Grant, Mrs Shepstone, Miss Lavinia Scott, Principal of Inanda
Seminary, Chief Luthuli.

Lyman K. Seymour High School

High School prefects with Mr and Mrs Jack Grant, 1951.

Adams College staff, *c*. 1954.

Adams Training College students, early 1950s.

Foundation stone ceremony at Adams Training College, 1953.

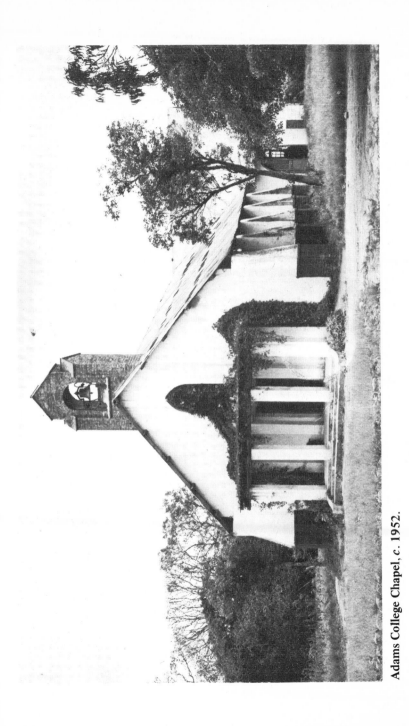

Adams College Chapel, c. 1952.

Farewell Service in the College Chapel, 1956. Dr Edgar Brookes at the lectern. Principal Jack Grant, the Revd A. F. Christofersen and the Revd Sivetye are seated below.

Mr Ballinger, M.P.[2] you were expecting to be able to do something to help me.

I hope very much you can, as poor little Lily is completely cut off now from her own people and rather in need of some contact with Bantu friends outside Adams College. She is a nice little thing and Mr Bomback tells me that he thinks she is practically certain to pass her Matriculation Examination at the end of the year, but she is rather bewildered at the new world into which she has come and tends in particular to rely far too much on me. I am meeting all her expenses until the end of 1951 but I cannot very well take the place of a close and intimate friend and companion. I really would not trouble you except that Mrs Macdonald told me you were intending to help her and would write to me on the subject.

In case you have mislaid my first letter I am enclosing a copy of it.

Yours very sincerely,
(Dr) Mabel Palmer

Encl.

Mary Lyon Hostel, Adams College
24/1/51

Dear Dr Palmer,

I received yours. Thanks for it. I am determined to do my duty – that is – to sit on my Matric studies and not to bring crimes upon you. I wouldn't like either to trouble you.

A shock to the college, I assume is that there should pass only two students out of a class of twenty-two and with only second grades, in Matric. That is why I would like to work hard from the onset.

---

who taught in the English Department and was also intimately connected with running classes for the non-European section of the University of Natal.

2. William Ballinger, who was in fact a Senator (1948–60), nominated to represent African interests in the Transvaal and Orange Free State. Born in Birmingham in 1894, he came out to South Africa in 1928 as adviser to the Industrial and Commercial Workers' Union. Like his wife, Margaret Ballinger (see above, p.84) he played a prominent, if conservative, role in trade union and liberal circles in South Africa, until his death in 1974.

N.E.E.D.—9

By the way I never told you I was ill from Rhuematism,[sic] now I understand that it is more serious because my feet, legs and knees are spurting where as I have sharp pain on my back.[1] If you wouldn't mind I wish to see the doctor there in Durban. I haven't told Mrs Bomback about my illness yet.

I shall tell you when I see the doctor what he says I'm suffering from.

With greetings and best wishes,

Yours sincerely,

Lily

P.S. I had a very pleasant weekend at Umbumbulu, with kind Miss Makhanya and all there.

Mary Lyon Hostel, Adams College,
28/1/51

Dear Dr Palmer,

Many thanks for the book you've sent me. I've started reading it.

I received your letter of the 18th instant. I replied it though I'm not sure whether you received it or not as the store post office burnt down the very day I posted it.

With all my heart I'm determined to do my work seriously and deligently. To sit on my studies and not to waste time. I don't want to bring you any crimes to solve nor do I want to disappoint you by failing, if God would help me in my wishes.

These days I'm not very well. I'm suffering from terrible rhuematism and cold. I understand I'm not well. I've told Mrs Bomback and she has advised me to see Dr Wilker[1] when the weather has been clear for some time, so that he would give me

1. Lily had been ill in hospital for some months — perhaps with rheumatic fever — during her Junior Certificate year at St Matthew's in the Ciskei. These pains remained undiagnosed, however. They could well have been symptoms of depression.

1. Dr Karl Wilker, the Head of the Training College, a Quaker. Primarily a psychologist, not a medical doctor, he had medical knowledge and attended to the needs of sick students. I am grateful to the unknown reader of the MS for the University of Natal Press for this information.

a slip to see a doctor in Durban if things are serious, as I've not sufficient money to send myself to Doctor in Durban.

When I came back from Umbumbulu I found Mrs McNeillage already got a girl, and I have worked at her place for eleven days. That is how I carried on. I started at 7.30 a.m. and she released me at (2 or 3) p.m. with a salary of 2/- a day. For four days I earned 2/6 for doing extra work. So I got £1. 6/- and including a 10/- I had sometime back asked from Mrs Bomback when I went with Mary, accompanying her to Durban, I had had a £1. 16/- which I used as ff:

£1. 16/-	
5/-	dress on sale for wearing at home (that is when not in school)
£1. 11/-	
5/-	nightdress on sale too, still good
£1. 6/-	
5/-	tennis shoes to help the school pair I've got
£1. 1/-	
8/8	Green wool (eight scales) for a jersey. I've sent the wool to a kind Miss Nellson[2] at Umbumbulu who has offered to make me a jersey quickly before the opening
12/4	
7/6	a coloured blouse to wear on at the Girls Department with my black skirt
4/10	and with the only 5/6 I had in my Post Office Saving book, (I saved in Umtata before I came here), I withdrew it :
10/4	
3/-	a vest
7/4	
4/-	a knicker
3/4	
1/3	writing pad
2/1	

2. Miss Nellson remains unidentified.

2/1	
6	envelopes
1/7	
6	stamps
1/1	
4	black polish
9	
3	bile pill
6	
6	white cotton
· ·	

I afraid I've not used it wisely enough but I urgently needed the articles. Next time I'll try to be more careful. With the Xmas present 10/- and this late one, I've bought a pair of white Sunday shoes for 19/9 (nineteen shillings, and ninepence). The dress, I had to buy it, as I gave the one I had been using to a poor girl as a New Year present. Moreover it had shrunk up and became too short and small for me. I had outgrown it totally. I couldn't even make out of it a blouse.

I had a pleasant time with kind Miss Makhanya, I felt homely[3] at her place.

With Greetings and Best Wishes,

I am,

Yours sincerely,

Lily

Adams College.
8/2/51

Dear Dr Palmer,

Many thanks for yours of the 3rd inst. and for the money. I am sorry to say that Dr Wilker couldn't give me a slip to see a doctor in Durban as the village doctor said he couldn't find anything wrong with me. Anyway I still intend to see the doctor there in Durban.

3. At home.

On the 5th I went to see Miss Makhanya and all at Umbumbulu. Mrs Makhanya, Miss Makhanya's mother, gave me provision and Miss Makhanya gave me a lovely bedspread. I'm really grateful to them in so much that I've bought them some little presents. I shall bring you a little present when I come to visit you (when you've invited me).

We have opened schools and have a new Dean[1] acting at Mrs Bomback's place. The formal opening day of our New Building[2] is on the 10th March. I'm busy with applications.

With greetings,

Yours sincerely,
Lily

P.S. Uniform is compulsory

The Girls Department, Adams College
16/2/51

Dear Dr Palmer,

Kindly excuse me for disturbing you so much. I wish to inform you that uniform this year is completely compulsory. I ask you if you would kindly help me with the articles I don't have, to complete my uniform. I haven't got the white Sunday frock, and the blazer.

I'm handing this letter to the New Dean to add on something. With Greetings,

I am,
Yours sincerely,
Lily

Dear Dr Palmer,

I like to mention that the blazer is not absolutely necessary. We have started work again at Adams College, and I am looking forward to a new years success.

Thank you!

Dean of Women
Elis. Kämper

1. Miss Elisabeth Kämper.
2. This was probably the Lyman K. Seymour High School, made possible through the benefaction of an American philanthropist.

145

Dear Dr Palmer,

Thank you very much for the letter you wrote me, and I'm very sorry to reply it rather late. The reason is that I'm not quite well and I feel depressed.

I had a very pleasant time indeed with Miss Makhanya at Umbumbulu. I always feel homely with her as much as I do when I visit you. I am grateful to you for introducing me to such a lady. What I most like of her she is not a hypocrite.

Forgive me for returning that book behind times. I'm sorry to say I have not finished it yet due to scarcity of time. I think I could follow it, and, I found it a very good book indeed. I hope you would lend me it again, probably next year.

We don't take any physical training here at our College. May I give you an outline of how we carry on our daily duties, so that you may have a little idea and be able to advise me where you think necessary.

We wake up at 5 a.m. and go for showers after which we start 'campus care' at 5.15 a.m. It takes 45 mins. now after Easter and before Easter it was an hour.[1]

This 'campus care' manual labour is either sweeping indoors or outdoors the ground around or raking or cutting long grass which is usually wet. I'm usually in cutting grass with sickles. There is no class distinction. We have to do the same type of work with Form I, the same time, irrespective of the amount of school work we ought to do in school.

Afterwards we go for breakfast and then to school which is over at 4.30 p.m. except on Wednesday (High School) – after lunch we don't return to school. Even that time has to be spent in some meetings such as 'Girl Guides'.[2] Of course I'm interested

1. In Edgar Brookes's day, and presumably also at this time, lessons began at 6.15 a.m., after this hour of manual labour (*A South African Pilgrimage*, 51).
2. For a fascinating account of the equivalent of the Girl Guide movement for Africans in the Transvaal, the mission dominated Girl Wayfarers association, and its objectives, see D. Gaitskell, ' "Upward all and play the game": the Girl Wayfarers' Association in the Transvaal, 1925–75' in P. Kallaway, *Apartheid and Education*, op.cit. American missionaries were amongst the most enthusiastic supporters of a movement which aimed at helping 'in

in 'Girl Guides' movement. Basket ball is played on Wednesday afternoons. We have one field and many students to practise. It is therefore obvious that weeks pass on without one taking part.

You can see that now that an physical excercise time is not available except when one runs for something, as we have to stick to our homework and studies when we get a free time.

I hope you will not be annoyed when I tell you of how we proceed. Of course I know you cann't do anything but to advise me. I mean you cannot rearrange how we should use time.

With greetings and best wishes,

I am,
Yours sincerely,
Lily

Adams College
18/4/51

Dear Dr Palmer,

Your letter received, many thanks for the pocket money. The new Dean of Women is Miss Kempa[1] from German.

That is how I spent last month's pocket money.

1.	Pillow case for	3/6	5.	stamps	6
2.	Lux soap	1/-	6.	lux face soap	8
3.	Aspro's	1/6	7.	blue	6
4.	ponds	1/6	8.	vaseline	6
	[face cream]			sweets	6

With greetings,

I am,
Yours sincerely,
Lily

P.S. Excuse me, I have no schooling shoes, please, and my size is '4'.   'The Same'

---

the adjustment to civilised conditions of these girls' and which 'would teach the right use of leisure, give wholesome discipline through teamwork and games, and inculcate loyalty to authority and the idea of sisterhood for service'. (From 'The Girls Wayfarers' Association of South Africa', n.d. cited in Gaitskell, 228.)

1. Elisabeth Kämper from Germany.

Dear Miss Kemper,

I wonder if you could allow Lily Moya with any friend whom she chooses to invite to come and spend a Saturday with me in Durban either May 12th or May 19th. My plan is that the two girls should come to my office behind Sastri College (Lily has been there) any time after 8.30. I would then hand them over to one of our newest graduates, a very nice dependable young woman called Gertrude Khanyile,[1] who would take them to see the sights of Durban; Lily specially wants to see the docks and they could go to the Museum and go round Durban on a bus top etc. They would then meet me for lunch at the Durban International Club, spend the afternoon there with me, and get back to Adams in the late afternoon. I think that would be a pleasant arrangement all round than for Lily to come to my house. She is so shy that I find her rather a trying guest. It is almost impossible to keep up a conversation. I will of course pay all her expenses.

And I think she had better have the college blazer she wanted, a friend of mine offered to knit her a jumper but tells me it won't be ready for some time and the cold weather will soon be on us. Also she says she needs another pair of shoes for school. Can you be so kind as to arrange to get these for her and include them in her next account? Or could you let me know where the blazer is to be obtained.

I hope I may have the pleasure of seeing you some day in Durban. My house is only a very little way off the road for anyone coming in from Adams, and if you would let me know a little in advance I should be delighted if you would come to lunch with me. Or perhaps it would suit you better to meet me in town for a cup of tea at my club – The Durban Women's Club in Stuttaford's Bdgs. I won't suggest the International Club, unless you would prefer it. But I expect it would be a

1. Unidentified.

148

relief for you to get away from inter-racial contacts, and relax in a purely European atmosphere.

With apologies for so long a letter,

I am,
Yours sincerely,
Mabel Palmer

Adams College
10/5/51

Dear Dr Palmer,

Glad to write to you. For today I'm writing you a very short letter. Recently, on Tuesday this week, I received a letter of invitation for June Holidays from a cousin and Aunt in Johannesburg, Sophiatown.[1]

I, therefore ask for your permission to allow me to spend the holidays with them. If you agree, please confirm that to the College Office as I cann't get concession or be allowed to go to Joh'burg without your consent.

With best wishes,
Yours very sincerely,
Lily

P.S. If you want to see the letter I shall bring it to you.

24 Clair Avenue, Durban
14 May 1951

Dear Lily

I am glad to learn that you have some relations in Johannesburg and think it would be a very good arrangement for you to spend the holiday with them. Only one thing bothers me and perhaps you will say that there is no need to worry. You are quite sure that this aunt and cousin are to be trusted – that they are not connected with your guardian and may be planning to send you back to him? How did they know where you are? You must remember that if by any unfortunate chance you fell

1. For Sophiatown, see the Epilogue, pp.142–3.

149

again into your guardian's power, we could not get you away from him.

There is no doubt that both Adams College and I myself are breaking the law in helping you to remove yourself from his custody and if he succeeded in re-establishing his control over you, nothing could be done. Our safe-guard is that he probably does not know where you are. But if these relations in Jo'burg know, how are we to be sure that he does not know also. We can protect you to some extent while you are at Adams or with Miss Makhanya but we could not protect you in Jo'burg.

However if you know this aunt and cousin well and are *quite* sure they are to be trusted, I think it would be a very good plan for you to visit them. Indeed it would be a relief to me to know that you had kind and reliable relatives. I am a v. old lady and will probably not be here long to help you.[1]

How will you manage about the fare to Jo'burg? And you would need warmer clothes than in Natal. I could lend you a warm muffler, one or two trifles like that, but I could not manage to give you a warm winter coat. I cannot afford at present to buy one for myself.

I hope I shall soon hear that you and a friend will be able to come in on May 26th, see the sights of Durban and have lunch with me at the International Club.

Yours v. sincerely,
Mabel Palmer

I should like to see the letter

Adams College
17/5/51

Dear Dr Palmer,

Thanks for such an early reply and for the pocket money. How they came to know of my address is a mystery I cannot tell.[2] Anyhow, I don't object to their invitation for God reveals

1. Mabel died in 1958.

2. In fact, Lily had been in touch with her family in Sophiatown all along. See Epilogue, p.142.

himself in many ways. I mean to say I shouldn't be self satisfied. I personally think a person like myself should never fail to hope for a good turning even at the worst of times. It is wise to attempt and meet new faces, and learn a lot from them, to renew spiritually and mentally. I don't mean to say I would tell them of my position.

After all it is a matter of few weeks. Should there be any sort of trick, I'll do my best to avoid it at its earliest possible. Then I shall wait and see if they send me a ticket (return). If they fail, I will fail too because after all it is a risk.

It is only yesterday that the Dean told me about your invitation 26th instant. She has said nothing about school shoes and blazer. I have to borrow the shoes from the other girl. I spent the last pocket money as follows:-

2/6 butter, as our diet is rather bad indeed
2/6 vicks, as cold is troubling me
2/6 cod liver oil
2/6 detiol, as I have rashes on the legs made by bugs which are so much troubling in 'Cawles' verander and the Study Hall − as the house is too old.[2]

You should be careful when writing the new Dean because she believes ruling with an iron hand. Perhaps it may be that she is still fresh from Germany, and does not know well how to deal with Africans.

Don't worry yourself much about the waistcoat and so on. You have done and still you are doing a great and unforgettable work for me. It is much you have done and doing for me that I wish we were about to close for December not June so as to give you too a release for such a burden.

There is that letter. Hope to hear from you soon.

I am,

Yours sincerely,

Lily

2. This list is interesting, both in its confirmation of the poor conditions students still had to endure, and because of the heavy expenditure on patent medicine: a sign that Lily was far from well. Cowles (misspelt 'Cawles' in the original) dormitory was named after a prominent American Zulu Mission family.

Wrote expressing doubt of intentions of aunt and cousin and warning Lily of danger of being forced back to custody of her guardian. Also confirming arrangements for June 2. M. Palmer

University of Natal, Durban
22nd May, 1951

The Principal,
Adams College.

Dear Mr Grant,

I am enclosing copies of my correspondence with the Native Commissioner of Umtata with regard to Lily.[1] You see that he does confirm the main outlines of her story.

When she arrived in Natal, I consulted Mr Havemann about her. Mr Havemann is the Chief Official in charge of the Native Affairs Department in Durban, and I always find him particularly interested and sympathetic. His advice was that we should lie low and not make any attempt to communicate with the people at Umtata.

Mr Bomback did, I believe write to the Magistrate, telling him where Lily was but never had an answer.

I hope you will not mind my suggesting that if you think of writing to the Magistrate again, it might be desirable to consult Mr Havemann first. He is not at his office at present, as he is engaged on zoning in Durban for the group areas arrangements,[2] but his home number is 49103.

I am not at all happy about this invitation to Lily from her Aunt, and I am enclosing for you a copy of a letter which I have written to her on the subject. It looks to me very suspicious that this invitation from the Aunt so closely follows the cousins visit to Umtata.

I had, however, occasion to ring up the Department of the Union Native Affairs, which deals with exemption from Native Law, and I asked the official who answered me, whether it was

1. See above, MP to NC, Umtata, 14.4.49 and NC to MP, 27.4.49.
2. In making arrangements for the racially segregated zones into which Durban was divided under the 1955 Group Areas Act.

possible to get Lily exempted from Native Law.[3] He said it would only be possible after she was 21 years and with the consent of the Guardian. But he assured me that she could not be compelled to marry the man whom her guardian chose, and that she had only to refuse her consent, and in that case, the marriage could not be held, but if the man got Lily once again under his care, I should be afraid he would find means to coerce her into giving her consent.

I am, in a way, a little sorry that I feel so doubtful about this invitation to her relations. It would be a great advantage if we knew she had relations to take charge of her if necessary. I am, after all 74 (just today) and of course I might pop off at any time.

I am intending, however, to make arrangements to make it available to pay for Lily this year and probably next. Meanwhile I enclose a cheque for 15/- for her Medical expenses.

One other thing. I forgot to put in that report on the objects of the Vacation School,[4] that it might be possible for lecturers who wished to hold joint meetings of their classes to do so, provided that they gave us adequate notice beforehand for time-table purposes. The others have agreed to the insertion of this sentence, and unless I hear from you to the contrary I shall assume that you also have no objection.

Yours sincerely,
(Dr) Mabel Palmer

Adams College
23.5.51

To: Dr M. Palmer,
Durban.

Dear Dr Palmer,

I am sorry that I have not answered your letter before but Mr Grant decided to write to you after there was another bad

3. In South Africa, the majority of Africans were (and are) governed by 'customary law', under which women are considered minors, subject either to their fathers or their husbands or guardians. Educated women could be emancipated from this perpetual 'minority' by a lengthy and complicated process. Legislation currently before Parliament will allow Black women to attain majority at 21 years which will remove the need for the emancipation.
4. For the black students of the University of Natal.

behaviour from Lily. At present she is making quite an effort, and I do hope she is realising that this is her last chance.

Mr Grant told me that you are prepared to have Lily and a friend on the 2nd of June, and I am quite sure that she will be delighted to go to Durban. I feel sorry for her as she has a difficult nature,[1] and finds it hard to settle down peacefully.

For your very kind invitation to visit you I thank you very much. I would indeed be very pleased to have this pleasure of meeting you in town. Yes, it would be a relief to relax in a purely European atmosphere, but so far I found many things to do and to organise, and soon we will have 'Esid laveleni'[2] in fairly good order with an improved garden in the near future I hope with an orchard.

Thank you again, and please forgive the delay. Mr Grant is I [know] hoping writing to you about Lily's holidays. We are anxious to know your decision, everything I can do to help I will certainly do, as I am staying during the vacation their may be the possibility,

> With kind greetings,
> Elisabeth Kämper

Regarding L. blazer, I think she is alright, she has a short woolen coat.

Adams College
1 June 1951

Dr Mabel Palmer,
Organiser, Non-European Section,
University of Natal, Durban.

Dear Dr Palmer,

Lily Moya

I am handing this letter to Lily for delivery to you, as I have not answered your letter of the 25.5. in time for the post.

---

1. For a discussion of Lily's 'difficult' nature, and what the term means, see Epilogue, p.205 below.
2. Esidlaveleni was the cluster of buildings used for girls' dormitories. It means 'The place where the houses are crowded together'. Again I am indebted to the unknown UN Press reader.

1st June 1951

Dr Mabel Palmer
Durban

> Dr to BOARD,
>   P.O. Adams Mission Station

Lily Moya

Fees for 1st and 2nd quarter	£10. 0. 0.
Books	14. 8.
	10.14. 8.
Shoes	1. 5. 0.
	£11.19. 8.

Note in Mabel Palmer's handwriting
There was an Adams College Blazer too £2.10. 0. I gave
directions that Lily was to leave that behind.

Receipt No. 5355.
P.O. ADAMS MISSION STATION   *25th June 1951*

Received from *Dr. Mabel Palmer.*

The sum of *Eleven pounds nineteen shillings and eightpence for*
fees, books and shoes.   *£11.19. 8.*

I have read and reread the correspondence which you enclosed. I have discussed it with Mr Dhlamini, one of Lily's teachers, and we support you in your contention that it would be unwise for Lily to go to Johannesburg.[1] Still, if she persists in going, after you also have advised her not to go, then I can refuse her readmission. Failing her trip to Johannesburg, I shall try to arrange a suitable place for her during the July holidays.

Lily will be going to Durban tomorrow. I have given her:
(a) Money to buy a pair of shoes – 25/-, for which she shall have to give me the receipt.
(b) An order on Ward & Salmon for a School Blazer.
Enclosed in this letter is Lily's account with the College for fees and books. This amounts to £10.14.8.

Yours sincerely,
G.C. Grant

University of Natal, Durban
2nd June, 1951

The Principal,
Adams College.

Dear Mr Grant,

For convenience in filing I am writing to you separately about Lily.

She duly arrived and has started on her sight seeing of Durban.

She seemed quite reconciled to not accepting the Johannesburg invitation, and I had a little talk to her generally on her behaviour.

An Indian friend of mine, Mrs Naidoo,[2] the wife of the man who was our Dean of Men last year, has sent down a large bundle

---

1. In fact, Mabel seems to have rather welcomed the idea initially. See above, MP to LM, 14.5.51.

2. Mrs Naidoo was the wife of Jack Naidoo, the registrar of M.L. Sultan Technical College, formerly on the teaching staff of Sastri College and part-time lecturer in Classics at the University of Natal in 1956. He would have been well known to Mabel through these activities, and their mutual interest in the Indian community in Natal. (See the biographical section in *The Indian as a South African*, edited by MP, published by the SAIRR, Johannesburg, to which they both contributed in 1956.)

of clothes for Lily, more I think than she can or ought to use herself.

I have told her to take about half, and she can give the others to her friends.

Perhaps you would like her to report to you what she has done about the clothes. They are really extremely nice and would be a boon to any poor girl. I have said that all the girls who receive this gift of clothing are to write to Mrs Jack Naidoo and thank her.

I hope Lily will now proceed on a more even keel. She is a good deal of trouble, but I think in the end it will be worth it.

Thanking you for your assistance in helping her,

I am,

Yours sincerely,
(Dr) Mabel Palmer

Letter handed personally to Lily Moya by Mabel Palmer

Adams College
3/6/51

Dear Dr Palmer,[1]

I meant to make my visit there yesterday, a pleasant and happy one, though internally I was heart broken, and cried alone the way back. It was not because I particularly like Durban (Town) but because of the thought of returning to Adams College, for various reasonable grievances.

I understand that I'm in a wrong type of school altogether, and my soul cann't get happiness and peace. All along I had been trying to take things as they are, but it is quite impossible. (a) There is totally lack of what is called real discipline. (b) Morality is wanting. I would not like to gain this world's riches but lose the essentialists[2] of a human being which differentiate him or her from sheep and goats in the face of the Lord, and the civilised world.

1. For comment on this extremely important letter, see Introduction, p.25.
2. Essentials.

(c) I don't need education which is barbarism under a camouflage.[3] I'm losing than gaining here, a lot too.

(2) Co-education is abominable when its foundation is not a proper one, like such schools as Mariniahill.[4]

(b) Liberty is good, but not a wordly one which interferes with other people who really hunger and thirst for righteousness and who are aimful and busy.

(c) I dont care much if a school is strict if it is on the right lines of education and proper civilisation.

(d) I have to leave Adams College one day and go into the world, I'm afraid, I'll have no space if I come from such a worldly place.

(3) I assume this place, in fact I suggest, is fit for deliquents only.

(a) A parent or a guardian who wishes or wants to reap a good crop, who really wants her daughter or adopted child fruitful results to his or her strenous struggle in educating her, should place her under good influence.

(b) I'm still a child student to be led by moral leaders, unbiasminded, and who takes his place as a calling to stand for and serve Jesus as a Christian in the true sense.

(c) Testing myself yesterday to another student of another school of my standard. I understood she was far better off in knowledge than myself and I have investigated why Adams College externals *always give bad results, yearly,* especially Matrics.[5] The parable of seeds and soil appeal to me a great lot. We are like those seeds sown in a barren soil, which shrink and perish, after a very short time.

(4) Another grievance is that there are very serious cases done by Adams students — but ignored. The only thing I have done is defending myself from a big girl too, who was not only disturbing me on my work, but also chasing me, the very girl I had been helping with my blouse last quarter for schooling, but, my

---

3. Introduction, note 68.
4. Mariannhill, the Roman Catholic school run by the Trappists.
5. The results at Adams were certainly poor: in December, 1950 only 2 students out of 22 were successful in the matriculation examination. St John's appears to have had a 60 per cent pass rate.

158

error has been magnified and has been badly dealt without justification.[6]

(5) If my Principal, Adams College, thinks that my going to Joh'burg is committing a crime, in so much that I cannot re enter the Adams College gates anymore, I think that this is a yoke or cross I should bear with joy, after because after all it is impossible to gain either civilisation or education in Adams College, especially when one is an external.[7]

I'm sorry to write finally such a letter about Adams. I know you really love this place and interested in its welfare, but, I cann't help. It is a fact, which if I hide it, as I had been all along trying to do so, would endanger both you and me, because I will fail the Exams and you would have wasted your precious money and time on me in Adams College, which thing I detest very much.

I understand that such schools as Inanda etc around are typical of what is meant [by] sound education and civilisation. That is all for today,

I remain,

Yours sincerely,

Lily

P.S. Excuse me for such a badly written and untidy letter I'm rushing for the time. There! the bell goes for supper.

The same

P.S. and I have never come across such raw school-boys as Adams students who have no respect who force and say anything they like to girls. As Form V class it is rot to the core in so much that I have lost pride of, and appetite on Adams College. I can be very glad if I can go to a school with no boys what-so-ever.

The same

---

6. This would seem to be Lily's answer to Miss Kämper's accusation of bad behaviour.
7. An outsider.

Dear Miss Makanya,

I enclose a letter from Lily which has really disturbed me a good deal and I don't know quite what to do about it. I flatly don't believe what she says about Adams College though there may be grains of truth in it here and there. I can quite imagine that some of the African boys are not as well behaved as they should be, and that Lily has been subjected to a certain amount of ill-natured teasing. But what does appear from the letter is that Lily whether for good reason or bad is so unhappy that she cannot work and that therefore all the money and time [I] have spent on her will be wasted. I feel rather inclined therefore to see whether they would take her next term either at Inanda or at Mariannhill.

I am afraid she is so maladjusted a type that she will probably have trouble wherever she goes — as she did at home and now at Adams. But perhaps she ought to be given another chance somewhere else. I feel that it is clear from her v. silly and ill-balanced letter that she will never make good at Adams. What do you think? If she failed to settle down at Inanda or Mariannhill, I would have nothing more to do with her.

I am sending you the letter for another reason, besides. As you are on the Council of Adams, you may like to consider whether there is any fragment of truth in Lily's charges. But please treat it as strictly confidential and return it to me. Under no circumstances let Mr Grant or any of the Adams College staff see it, as that would be an end of Lily at that school. And I do not know yet if it might be possible to get her in anywhere else.

I do apologise for troubling you again, but Lily is really beginning to be rather too much for me. I am sorry now I ever gave her any help or encouragement at all.

Yours sincerely,
Mabel Palmer

Dear Lily,

You *are* a little nuisance. It is most disappointing to receive a letter like the one you wrote me this week, just after I thought you were settling down at last and after I had gone to a good deal of trouble to give you a pleasant and interesting day in Town.

I am really at a loss what to do about it. Other people are happy at Adams and I can't see why you should not be. You take the teasing of the other students too seriously, you think far too much of yourself and your own judgment. I don't at all believe that your sweeping and vague charges about Adams are justified, though no doubt there are some things that are not quite as they should be and that ought to be put right — that is true of any institution.

I repeat I don't know what to do, and shall have to consider and ask advice of several people.

But there are two things I can say at once. You are simply silly in saying that Mr Grant thinks it wicked of you to want to visit your own relations. If we were sure that this aunt and cousin would not betray you to your guardian we would be delighted that you should go. But I think it far too much of a risk. I did not care for the tone of your cousin's letter and you seem to know very little about this cousin or aunt. At all events you have sent me no details as to how well you know them, and how often you have seen them. Both I and Mr Grant and Mr Dhlamini are inclined to think their invitation is a trick to get you back into your guardian's power and we do not think that such a risk should be taken. But nobody thinks or will think you 'wicked' in this connection only too innocent and unsuspicious — *not* wise and sensible.

The other thing is — in your letter you use the phrase 'adopted daughter'. I don't know if you were thinking of me and yourself when you used those words, but I feel I must make it plain that I do not and will not regard you in any such light and that I have never said anything to justify you in believing so. I was interested in your letters and sympathetic towards a girl struggling for better education, and I felt it was up to me to give you some help. That help I will give (unless it becomes clear that you cannot be helped) for this year and perhaps for next if it seems necessary that you should add a teacher's training course to your Matric. But what I want is that you should as soon as possible be in a position to stand on your own feet. Also as a rather forlorn little protegee I will from time to time see you for a talk and arrange for you small treats like the one planned for Saturday. But beyond that I will not go and every time you press on me a desire for a more intimate relation you really force me back into reserve and guardedness in dealing with you. I am v. sorry for you and v. anxious to help you to an independent and satisfactory life, but any close or intimate friendship between us is really not possible and you will only spoil things if you grasp at it. But this doesn't mean that I am not interested in you or do not want to be kind to you; I *do* within due limits.

You talk a good deal of your prayers. Do you ever pray to be made more humble and less self-righteous, more adaptable and more sensible?

I haven't at all come to any decision about you, but I should think far more highly of you if you showed stamina enough to adapt yourself to Adams for the remainder of this session?

Yours v. sincerely,
Mabel Palmer

Adams College
8/6/51

Dear Dr Palmer,[1]

Hearty thanks for the clothes you have given me and for the blanket. Please express my thanks also to Mrs Naidoo and to Miss Makhanya for the trouble she took on and kindness she showed on me, in taking me round.

I have received your latest letter. What I said to you was sincere. I have taken quite a long time in thinking over this matter. In the first place forgive me for the paper I have used, at present I cann't get a lighter paper, and our ink is all the same, because we use bottled inks as ready made in our High School, and there is no ink powder.

1. For comment on this letter, see Introduction, p.30.

162

All the while I had been wondering why almost all students were like this to me. I now speak confidentially to you. The source of all my troubles is Mr Dhlamini, a teacher in the High School.[2] Some sympathetic students have come to confess it to me. He has given them instructions not to walk with me.

He has went to the Dean and said that the biggest liar in this College is Lily. I have been told by students. The girl with whom I quarrelled was advised by him, and she even said it out, there are some girls to whom she said, she should say anything about me to the Dean and Principal he will stand for her and nothing can happen in this College beyond his word. Whenever he saw me walking with a student he called that student to his office and advised him against me.

The girls who turned against me on the last Saturday during the holidays were hired by him so that I may gain notority and be injured.

He has some girls he gives large sums of money and some special food to influence the Dean and to bring to him as much lies as he wishes to anybody whom he fears may reveal his evil actions.

I didn't know that he said in my report I was nervous, I have been informed that he said so because he wanted whatever ever I report to you should be taken simply whether serious and that you (in Durban, etc) should assume that it is because I am nervous.

He has insisted boys to be rude to me and even swear or push me. He has insisted them also to cross question me. How did I come to know of you and how many other Departmental people I know. How is it that I came immediately after strike?[3] and he says he didn't know about me.

Dr Palmer you best know me. I have corresponded with you from 1949. How I came to know about you is no students business. A letter you write about me passes to the students.

I am sorry to be so persistive[4] about this. It is not that I had not been realising, but that I thought it best and wise to take time and then proves have been given to me.

---

2. A pseudonym.
3. The food boycott and expulsion of students in August 1950.
4. Persistent.

I have never said that I was going to Joh'burg to any of the students but they have advised me that Mr Dhlamini has convinced the Principal that I shouldn't go. They have warned me because they say it is more of a second plot, and they say he is cock sure that I will not go according to his words.

If that is really true that Mr Dhlamini has convinced that I should not go what relation is he as to where I should spend my holidays.

As long as he is convincing everybody what an evil child I am as well as students. I say perhaps he may live or they may leave[5] a happier life when I've left.

That is all for today,

I am,
Yours sincerely,
Lily Moya

P.S. The rest of the clothes I think do not fit me, I'll give them to some other needy school-children in other places.

Umbumbulu
8th June, 1951

My dear Dr Palmer,

I have your letter and Lily's to you which I am enclosing. Well, in view of the unhappiness Lily is experiencing I agree with your suggestion: to give her another and last change — transfer her to Inanda or Mariannhill.

I am wondering why she wanted to go to Jo'Burg. The expense that would be connected with the trip. Who would bear that?

I shall keep it all confidentially, as you requested.

I do not think Adams is as bad as Lily paints it. I am sure the boy students did not mean an ill by their teasing stunts. In my days at Adams they use to tease us girls and even now my school-mates, of those still, tease me when we meet and call me by nicknames they had given me.

5. Live.

Lily must forget herself sometimes or else she will not be happy even in her ideal school. I am very sorry that she should burden you so much with the knocks few people escape.

If I can help call upon me, Dr Palmer,

Yours sincerely,
Sibusisiwe Makhanya

University of Natal, Durban
8th June, 1951

Miss Lily Moya,
Adams College.

Dear Lily,

Mrs MacDonald has kindly presented you with a blanket which I have sent to you per parcel post. It is very kind of her and I hope you will write to her and thank her for it.

Her address is:- P.O. Box 110, Westville.

I hope the clothes that Mrs Naidoo sent fit you nicely, or at least that you will be able to alter them so they do.

With very cordial greetings,

I am,
Yours sincerely,
Dr Mabel Palmer

Dictated before I got your letter

Adams College
12 June 1951

Dr Mabel Palmer,
Organizer Non-European Section,
University of Natal, Durban.

Dear Dr Palmer,

Lily reported back safely. When the clothes arrived, she took them to the Dean whom she consulted about the distribution. I enclose two letters from the girls who benefitted.

165

The Tenniquoit net and quoit arrived safely and these have been handed over to the Dean who will see that they find good use.[1]

Greetings and thanks to Mrs MacDonald and yourself,

Sincerely,

Jack Grant[2]

Adams College
13/6/51

Dear Dr Palmer,

Thank you very much for yours of the 8th inst. I am highly grateful to you for introducing me to your friends and it is very kind of them to help me.

This blanket is very lovely and as for the clothes they are lovely and fit me well too except for one blouse which of course I know what to do with it.

It deems me highly expedient to ask you to permit me to spend my June Holidays in Johannesburg with Aunt and cousin who invited me. Cousin and his sisters had shown no malevolence to me till they had to leave for their home people in Johannesburg where I suppose are proceeding in their educations.

After all they know what sort of a person my guardian is, as they themselves had conflicts with him too, though they weren't staying with him.

I am also writing Mrs MacDonald today. I hope my writing is a little bit clearer today.

With best wishes,

Yours very sincerely,

Lily Moya

P.S. Please tell me. What would you really like me to be, a nurse, a teacher or a writer or something else?, as from next year.   'Same'

---

1. The gift was typical of Mabel's practicality and thoughtfulness; it may have been a response to Lily's remark (4.4.51) that there was no physical education at Adams.
2. G.C. Grant.

You have helped very much, and saved me from the greatest difficulties which would have ruined the rest of my life, so, don't you think next year I should start working and gain some living. If I would be a nurse I would like to be trained at MacCord's Hospital. Kindly reply me.

University of Natal, Durban
15th June, 1951

Sister Edista,
Head Teacher,
P.O. Mariannhill.

Dear Sister Edista,

I wonder if you could give me any help in a difficulty which is confronting me?

I am paying for the education of a rather unfortunate little girl aged about eighteen from Umtata.

She wrote to me telling me how much she wanted to get away to school, and that her Guardian and Uncle (she is an orphan) refused to send her.

I entered into negotiations with Adams about her, and then she rather precipitated matters by running away and making her way to Adams where she had a vague idea that I was to be found. That was in September last year.

She is working for the Matriculation examination, but unfortunately she has never settled down. She is a difficult person, intensely egotistical and rather inclined to believe that people conspire to make things difficult for her, and I have just learnt that she is very unhappy and that she feels unable to work and is most anxious to be removed from Adams.

I think her difficulties are mostly her own fault, but I am pretty sure that in her present state of mind she will be quite unable to do justice to herself.

She has, by the way, a quite marked gift in writing. What really attracted me to her first was her clever and interesting letters.

Would it be possible for her to be admitted to Mariannhill for the second term? The subjects she has been working on are

English, Mathematics, Zulu, Geography, Botany, Zoology and Agricultural Science. That is seven subjects and of course she would only need six.

I imagine too that she will probably have to have a teachers' training on top of her Matriculation before she can really begin to earn enough to stand on her own feet, and you have, I know, a Teachers' Training Course.

She is an Anglican by Religion, and apparently very devout, though her religion does not help her to the humility of a young student. But I am very sorry for her. She is an unfortunate and unhappy little creature and I feel that she should be given a second chance.

If you wish for any further information, perhaps you would ring me at 888415 on Monday, and on Tuesday (but I hope I may hear from you before Tuesday) at 28982.

I am also communicating with Inanda, and it seems possible that Miss Scott[1] would consent to take her, but I feel that it might be desirable for her to go to a school which is not under the American Mission Board, so that she can make a completely fresh start, and I am inclined to think that the religious atmosphere of Mariannhill would suit her better than the agressively Protestant attitude of the American Board Schools.

The one objection to Mariannhill is that she has a curious antipathy to boys and men, and thinks she would prefer an exclusive girls school, but I imagine that at Mariannhill you keep the boys and girls rather carefully separate.[2]

I would be paying all her expenses and be responsible for her in the holidays. She would probably go to Miss Mkanaya's place near Umbumbulu, but I should like her to earn some money during the vacation if possible, as she is a little too much inclined to think that I am made of money (which is far from being the case) and can meet her needs without the slightest difficulty.

I do not wish to deny that this is a difficult case, but as I say, I think she should be given a second chance, and it seems to

1. Miss Lavinia Scott, Principal of Inanda.
2. See Introduction, pp.24ff.

168

me quite possible that Mariannhill would be the most suitable place for her to have that second chance.

With apologies for troubling you, and kind regards.

I am,
Yours sincerely,
(Dr) Mabel Palmer

St Francis' College
Girls' Department
P.O. Mariannhill
18th June, 1951

Dear Dr Palmer,

I found your letter in the late afternoon when I came back from College.

I have consulted Sr. Lucia who is the Head Teacher of the High School Dept. We are willing to give the girl a trial. We can, however, keep her only if she fits in and submits to school discipline. We shall do our best to make her feel at home. She need not fear the boys; our Girls' Dept. is quite separate from that of the boys. We offer all the subjects you mention.

This letter will leave here only Tuesday morning. I hope you will have it in the afternoon.

Kind regards,
Yours sincerely,
L.M. Edista, C.P.S.

Adams College
20 June 1951

Dr Mabel Palmer,
Organizer, Non-European Section,
University of Natal, Durban.

Dear Dr Palmer,

Lily Moya

After further consideration I regret that I shall not be able to find accommodation at the College for Lily during the forth-coming holidays. The reason is that she is not able to live

169

amicably with one of the two other girls who will be staying at the College. Please therefore make other arrangements for her.

Yours sincerely,
G.C. Grant,
Principal

Telephone message *20th June 1951*

Miss Scott phoned and said that she had been in touch with Mr Grant, and found that Lily is in her second year matric. and that if she were responsible for the girl she would be inclined not to move her midterm just before matric.

The subjects offered at Inanda are not quite the same as those Lily is taking at Adams – they offer domestic science instead of agricultural science, and geography is taken at the same time as mathematics, so that Lily would have to find something to replace geography, which may be difficult at this late hour.

Miss Scott says that Mariannhill offer a larger range of subjects, and I said I did not think you had heard yet from Mariannhill, and would probably phone Miss Scott – Inanda 1 – after you had heard from Mariannhill.[1]

Community Centre, P.O. Umbumbulu
21st June, 1951

Dear Dr Palmer,

I am wondering what Lily's plans are for the coming vacation. Is she still intent on going to J.H. Burg? Mrs Hosken[2] told me some five weeks ago that she (Lily) was booking for Johannesburg. Of course, I have not breathed a word to anyone concerning the correspondence you sent me.

With kind regards,
Yours sincerely,
Sibusisiwe Makhanya

1. The 'I' referred to here is Mabel's secretary, who took the phone message.

2. Mrs Julia Hosken was the Secretary at Adams, and one of the few members of the staff to speak Zulu. She was also a close friend of Sibusisiwe's, and on the Council of the Umbumbulu Social Centre.

Dear Lily,

I hope you have realised by this time how very silly your letter about Mr Dhlamini[1] was. I shall simply ask a series of questions:

1) Why should a busy teacher go out of his way to annoy one of his pupils? Hasn't he dozens of things to do and think about more important to him than that?

2) Why in particular should he instruct other students to pump you? If he wanted to know how I came to help you, he could learn that much more easily by asking Mr Grant or even by asking me. I have known Mr Dhlamini for a number of years and there is no reason why he should not approach me himself. But in any case there is no special drama or mystery about it. There must be dozens or even hundreds of girls in the world who are being helped with their education by kindly patronesses as I was helped myself by Mrs Bernard Shaw.

3) Why should he not state his opinion about your visit to Johannesburg when consulted by Mr Grant? and why should not Mr Grant consult him? He is at once your teacher and a Bantu appreciating the power of Bantu custom as it is difficult for us Europeans to do.

4) When the other students told you Mr Dhlamini was prompting the baiting of you, do you not think they were just making fun of you, trying to see how much you would swallow, if your self-inflated idea of your own importance?

I am bound to say that having known Mr Dhlamini for some time and knowing too the esteem in which he is held by other people, I find it very hard to credit the statements in your letter. And you should be very careful of making them public in any way. I should imagine they are libellous and that Mr Dhlamini could bring a legal action against you for uttering them if indeed he were to think it worth noticing what a not v. sensible and disgruntled school-girl said about him. That letter was intensely disagreeable to me and I hope I shall have no more of this sort of thing. Come now! Pull yourself together. Use your

1. See above, LM to MP, 8.6.51.

common-sense. Try to realise that *you* are not the centre of the world and that people have lots of other things to do, rather than conspiring to annoy and injure you. You have come to see things out of focus and so you create unreal miseries and distresses for yourself. It is no wonder people think you don't speak the truth, if you conjure up such imaginative nightmares. When you go to Mariannhill, you must try to see things as they are, and not in the light of an undue sense of your own importance.

Yours v. sincerely,
Mabel Palmer

24 Clair Avenue, Durban
21 June, 1951

Dear Miss Scott,

Thank you for all the trouble you have taken about Lily. But I have nearly come to the conclusion that she had better go to Mariannhill, where they offer all the courses she has been taking at Adams. Also I think it may be easier for her to make a new start in a completely new atmosphere where nothing could be known about her mistakes at Adams.

I am going down to Adams to see her and Mr Grant (or his deputy) on Monday next and then I will let you know finally. But unless something quite unforeseen crops up – and it always may with Lily – I shall send her to Mariannhill. Another advantage would be that she could take her Teachers' Training Course also at Mariannhill.

But all the same I am much obliged to you for the trouble you have taken to give me all the necessary information.

Yours v. sincerely,
Mabel Palmer

Lily is taking:		Inanda offers:	
	English		English
	Maths		Maths
	Zulu		Zulu
	Geo		History
	Botany		Botany
	Zoology		Zoology
	Ag. Science		Domestic Science

172

Dear Miss Makanya,

I have decided to send Lily to Mariannhill; they are willing to take her and offer all the courses she has been studying whereas at Inanda they do not offer the courses and it would be difficult for her to start another subject at this stage. I do hope she will be happier there; I am quite sure I should not. But it may be that a stricter, more Catholic atmosphere will suit Lily better. At all events I think she must be got away from Adams. I have had another letter from her, which has really disgusted me, making the most preposterous charges against a staff member — charges absurd on the face of it.

But there remains the question of what to do with her in the holidays; it is really almost impossible for me to have her here and if I did it would intensify her false views of the relationship between herself and me. Could you possibly take her? I will of course pay whatever you think proper. But it would really be better for her to do some work in July, at least in return for her board. I would be most grateful to you, if you could arrange something of that sort.

I am sorry I didn't tell you about her plan for going to Johannesburg. She has an invitation from an aunt and cousin who apparently are prepared to pay her fare. But I wonder if it is not a trick to get her back into her guardian's control for the sake of her lobola. I can't be sure of course but it seems to me a risk not worth running especially as the aunt or cousin have just returned from a visit to Umtata. I told Mr Grant what I thought and he consulted Mr Dhlamini who agreed. So Mr Grant told her he could not prevent her going to Johannesburg, but he could refuse to re-admit her to Adams and he would take that line. I feel bound to back him up. But I have told her that if we can get any indication that the aunt and cousin are *not* in league with the guardian I would let her go at Xmastime. I wonder if it would be possible to make some enquiries in Jo'burg. Of course if these relations were all right and wouldn't give Lily away to her guardian, I would be only too delighted to let her go to them.

I am coming out to Adams on Mon. aft. (Mrs McDonald is being kind enough to bring me) and we might have time to come on and see you. But that would depend on Mrs MacDonald's arrangements. In the meantime, I should be grateful for a speedy answer or even a phone call. I'll be at the office till 5 tomorrow (Friday) and till 1 p.m. on Saturday 28982 and at other times at home 888415.

With many apologies for bothering you, and many thanks for your kind help.

Yours v. sincerely,
Mabel Palmer

POST OFFICE TELEGRAPHS REPLY PAID

To: SIBUSISIWE MAKHANYA
     UMBUMBULU

CAN MRS MACDONALD AND I COME TO LUNCH WITH YOU ON MONDAY 25TH JUNE

MABEL PALMER
24 Clair Avenue,
Durban

24 Clair Avenue, Durban
21 June 1951

Dear Lily,

I am sorry I have been some time in answering your letters, but I have been v. busy with university work and have had to leave my private letters for the time being. You are not the only correspondent I have been forced to neglect I can assure you.

I have practically decided to send you to Mariannhill next term; at Inanda they do not offer the courses you have been taking. Sister Edista, the Principal of the Girls Department has written a v. kind letter, which I will show you. I am coming down to Adams on Monday afternoon to complete the arrangements about your transfer and the July holiday. I continue to feel that I cannot approve of your going to your aunt and cousin until I have more evidence that their invitation is not a trick to get you back under your guardian's control. I have

174

asked Miss Makhanya to take you and I hope she will agree.

There will be three conditions for my sending you to Mariannhill 1) you must not gossip about Adams or your treatment there. If asked why you left, you must say simply that you were never very well at Adams and that it was thought a change might be good for your health.

2) You must not mention me to your fellow-students. Goodness knows I don't like making a mystery of so simple a thing as the help I am giving you, but apparently you put the other students against you at Adams by boasting about your relation to me and I think it will be safer for you to say nothing about it.

3) You must not complain to me about the treatment you get at Mariannhill and you must realise that if you have any trouble with the school authorities I will not interfere, except to back up their decisions. If you cannot make good at Mariannhill, I shall come to the conclusion that my help is not doing you any good and will be compelled to withdraw it. But if you can settle down and be happy there I will finance you also for the year of teacher-training.

That brings me to the question of what you are to be. Within your limits of choice, I think you should be guided by your own wishes. It is a decision that will affect your whole future life, and for the sake of getting earlier employment you should not take up an occupation that is not congenial to you. Of course your field of choice is not wide. As far as I can see, it is as follows:

1) *Medicine*, if you can get a Second class Matric. But I don't think somehow that you would make a good doctor.

2) *Nursing*. But you have told me that that does not attract you.

3) *Teaching*. The advantage of this is that good teachers can get jobs without much difficulty and that it would leave spare time for writing or for further education on the University level, you certainly could not keep yourself as a writer for many years, if ever. But you have a gift in that direction, if you can cease to be so intensely interested in yourself, and can achieve a detachment that will enable you to depict the lives of others as vividly as you can describe your own personal experiences.

There are other occupations, librarianship, social work,

commercial worker (short-hand, type-writing and accounts) etc. but I fear the openings for Bantu girls in these directions are v. limited. On the whole teaching is most easily accessible for you, and would give you leisure to try your hand at writing. At first you would almost certainly be unsuccessful and you would have to keep on persevering for a long time before your MSS were accepted by editors and for a much longer time before you could make a living by writing.

But you must decide for yourself. My one piece of advice is don't try anything really uncongenial to you. I will get you all the information which you want, if I can.

I haven't had time to re-read all your letters. But if I have left anything out, you can remind me of it on Monday.

I do hope this change will be beneficial to you and that you will be happy and do well at Mariannhill.

Yours v. sincerely,
Mabel Palmer

I can read your recent letters much more easily, thank you.

24 Clair Avenue, Durban
21 June, 1951

Dear Sister Edista,

Thank you for your prompt reply to my letter and for your offer to take Lily. I have practically made up my mind to accept it with many thanks. It will be a great advantage to her to be able simply to continue with the courses she was already doing at Adams and if it is decided that she is to be a teacher she could stay with you another year for the teacher-training.

I am going down to Adams to see her on Monday and will let you know definitely after that. And you will let me know about the clothes and equipment she will need.

I will explain to her that she *must* accept the school's discipline and arrangements generally and must not complain to me about anything she dislikes. Also I shall make it a condition that she does not mention the fact that I am helping her. She seems to have boasted about it at Adams and that seems to have set the other girls against her.

176

I do hope she will make the best of this new chance. If she does not I shall just have to give her up and send her back to her own people.

With very many thanks for your kind help in what was really a difficult situation.

I am,

Yours sincerely,

Mabel Palmer

The Community Centre

P.O. Umbumbulu

28/6/51

Dear Dr Palmer,

There is the blazer returned as your suggestion. I couldn't give them myself. I was really afraid to do such a thing, and I would have been acting more of a lunatic than would it be good manners.[1]

Please hand it back and ask them yourself to give you the money.

Dr Palmer, I have nothing to put on. It is extremely cold. You talked of some work and I'm not sure what you really wanted me to do. I'm as usually happy with Miss Makhanya, but, I would like to do some work if I cann't go to Joh'burg.

I am,

Yours sincerely,

Lily Moya

P.O. Umbumbulu

29th June, 1951

Dear Dr Palmer,

Lily seems happy. I think she'll appreciate the arrangements you mentioned you were making for her as from the 20th of July. I have not said anything to her about them.

We did look for your spectacles and were disappointed not

---

1. Lily was so angry (lunatic — 'mad'), that she could not trust herself to act civilly towards the teachers at Adams in handing over the blazer herself. (See MP to Miss Kämper, 30.7.51.)

[to] find them where the car was but now we are happy of the report 'Lost and Found'.

I enjoyed your call you made on us Monday.

Yours sincerely,
Sibusisiwe Makhanya

Adams College
29.6.51

Dear Dr Palmer,

This is just a short note letting you know that Lily left the College on Tuesday after she had been told to leave on Wednesday. She was definitely rude when I gave her the message which came from the office that she should go to Miss Mhakanya on Wednesday. She did not tell me when she was going but just packed and went off. I am sorry to say that instead of improving in her behaviour she did exactly as she liked and proved to be very disobedient.

With best wishes to yourself,

I am,
Yours sincerely,
Elisabeth Kämper

24 Clair Avenue, Durban
2 July 1951

Dear Sister Edista,

I am very glad to accept your kind offer to enrol Lily Moya in your Matric. class for next term. I hope she will be happier with you than she was at Adams.

1)   Would you let me know when the next term starts.

2)   Whether Lily will need any special equipment in the way of clothes etc.

3)   What books you use in the classes of English, Mathematics, Zulu, Geography, Botany, Zoology and Agricultural Science? I hope they may be the same as her existing textbooks, as I certainly don't want (if it can be avoided) to have to spend a lot of money on new books for her.

4)   What your fees are and when payable?

I should be very grateful for a speedy answer at least to

HIGH SCHOOL — ADAMS COLLEGE

Report to parent on *Lily Moya*   *June 1951*

Number in Class *28*   Class position *20*

	Marks obtained	Minimum for pass	Maximum		Teachers' remarks
English	*135*	*133*	*400*	*34%*	*Weak*
Vernacular	*106*				
Geography	*78*	*117*	*350*	*22%*	*Weak. A lazy student*
Zoology/ Arithmetic	*137*	*117*	*350*	*40%*	*Satisfactory*
Biology/Science	*176*	*117*	*350*	*45%*	*Satisfactory*
Mathematics	*105*	*133*	*460*	*28%*	*Good. Can do better than this*
Latin/Afrikaans					
Agriculture	*207*	*117*	*350*	*59%*	*F. Good*
TOTAL	*867*	*780*			

N.B. Marks below 25% of possible maximum in each subject are not
included in the aggregate.

CONDUCT   *Not always satisfactory*   *E. KAMPER*   DEAN
          Fair   *R. KEET*   FORM MASTER

REMARKS   *Capable but sometimes careless and rather concerned with
          herself. Conduct can be better.*

          B.M. MTSHALI   HEAD MASTER

School re-opens   *1st August.*   Fees etc. outstanding
N.B. Students owing fees etc. cannot be re-admitted when school re-opens
in August. Your attention is drawn to this.

Needs to throw herself into her work more fully.
W.H. ROBERTS for PRINCIPAL

No. 1. as I have a plan for her to spend a few days in Durban with a Bantu family who are friends of mine, before she goes on to Mariannhill.

I am very grateful to you for undertaking to have her.

Yours very sincerely,
Mabel Palmer

24 Clair Avenue, Durban
8 July, 1951

Dear Miss Makanya,

I hope you don't disapprove of my decision to let Lily go to Johannesburg. I was never very happy about Mr Grant's attitude, but as long as Lily was at Adams, I was bound to back him up. I hoped we might convince her that it was unwise to go, but if she insists and says that there is a death in the family, and that they want her in connection with that, I felt I had to let her go. I am still not sure that it is not a trick to get her back under the control of her family, but to tell the truth, I shall not be very sorry if it is. She behaved very badly when she left Adams, disobeying the order that she was to leave on Wednesday and departing secretly on Tuesday, after being v. rude to Miss Kamper. Her report is not at all satisfactory and I can't think she can pass Matric in November, and what to do with her if she doesn't I really don't know. In fact I am becoming v. sorry that I ever undertook to help her.

However if she comes back I shall give her the rest of the year at Mariannhill. I think she must have tried to phone me last night. Twice the bell rang but when I went there was no answer. I think it must have been Lily trying to put through a call from a call-office.

I think I must apologise for having on one or two occasions suggested that you should phone me. I hadn't any idea that the phone was 2 miles away and that it would mean a four-mile journey for you. I thought it was only a few hundred yards away from you. In future if I need to contact you in a hurry, I shall wire.

With many thanks for your kind co-operation in regard to Lily and hoping to see you before long.

Yours v. sincerely,
Mabel Palmer

Dear Dr Palmer,

Enclosed please find an Application form and Prospectus; the latter answers your questions re school equipment, fees, etc.

As regards .books, I spoke to Sr. Lucia. If it is not inconvenient, she would like that Lily comes over one day. She could then talk to the girl and find out how far she has gone in the various subjects, the kinds of books she uses, etc. It might be advisable for Lily to copy some notes which the students have taken during the first term so that she has a proper start when school begins on August 1st. Sr. Lucia thinks that Lily could perhaps come one week earlier; she may also come any day now and go back when she is through with her work. Lily must send in or bring along a transfer card from the Principal of Adam's College.

Yours sincerely,
Sister Edista, C.P.S.

Umbumbulu
10th July, 1951

Dear Dr Palmer,

Lily's people have not sent the money for her Johannesburg trip. I have had a straight talk with Lily — told her she cannot act as though she was independent — already working and earning a salary. She is still dependent on others and should co-operate with people like you and others.

Please do not 'worry' about her. I am handling the situation. Today and yesterday she is nice and bright. Well, the promised money has not come! She can only blame her relatives for that.

With kind regards,
Yours sincerely,
Sibusisiwe Makhanya

P.S. If this 'wonderful' Johannesburg trip plans end by not materialising are you still planning to have her spend part of the last 10 days with Mrs Selby Ngcobo as you previously suggested? I think it would be nice for her. I have not said anything to her about it, of course. S.M.

24 Clair Avenue, Durban
12 July, 1951

Dear Miss Makanya,

I am v. sorry to learn from your phone message last night that Lily was behaving so badly. It is really inexcusable after all your kindness and I shall insist on her apologizing to you. I rather expected her some time to-day, but she has not appeared. I have now heard definitely from Mariannhill about her. School opens on Aug. 1st, but they want her to go a week earlier, so as to have some opportunity of linking on to the class-work. I think she had better come and spend the day with me on Monday and I can fix things up then. Please tell her to bring my books and the names of all her school books. They would like her to visit them at Mariannhill as soon as possible. I wish I could go with her but I should have to have a car and I can't v. well ask Mrs MacDonald again. So I am afraid Lily will have to make a second visit for that. I will try to arrange for her to go to the Ngcobo's if possible. But after the rudeness and lack of consideration she has shown you, I almost hesitate.

I am really getting tired of her tantrums and am feeling quite ready to send her back to Umtata under escort to be returned to her guardian. However we'll give her another chance at Mariannhill. Let me know if by any chance she can't come on Monday. Wednesday might do, but *not Tuesday*, I have to be at the office that day.

I shall expect her on Monday then unless I hear from you.

With many regrets that you have had so much trouble,

Yours v. gratefully,

Mabel Palmer

Phone conversation 16 July 1951
Mr Havemann's advice re Lily

1) Not to be too disturbed if she disappears. Durban is full of Bantu girls who have run away from their guardians and most of

them manage all right, get employment in factories and as domestic workers.

2)   If information is required as to aunt write to:
    Superintendent, Welfare Dept.
    Non-European Affairs Deptmt.
    Municipality of Johannesburg
    His Majesty's Buildings, Johannesburg.

3)   If I want to send her back to her guardian, write to Magistrate, Umtata, saying I will pay the cost of the journey, or the guardian can come and get her.

24 Clair Avenue, Durban
23 July, 1951

My dear Lily,

This letter is to let you know finally that I have decided not to continue to pay for your education. My reasons are:

1)   Your report (a copy of which I enclose) is very poor — I don't think you have any chance of passing Matric in November, and it would be years before you complete the Matric and the Teacher training. I am not in a position to continue to support you for so long though had you worked and done well at school, shown yourself sensible of the sacrifices I was making on your behalf I would have made an effort to continue the support I was giving you.

2)   The fact that wherever you go you cause trouble. I was shocked to learn from Miss Kamper that you were disobedient and rude on Tuesday, after all the trouble I took to talk to you on Monday. I enclose a copy of Miss Kamper's letter. Then you upset all the peace of Miss Makanya's house by your inconsiderate behaviour.

3)   Lastly, you treated me with great lack of courtesy and gratitude in not keeping your appointment to see me on Monday morning and in never communicating with me in any way since.

I am sorry that our association should terminate in this way — though I am not sorry to be no longer responsible for you — but it cannot be helped.

Will you please send me back my books

1)   Alcott. Little Women

2) Stark. Letters from Syria
3) Baker. First Woman Doctor.
And also the sheet and blankets which you, shall we say, borrowed from Miss Makanya.

I shall still be interested in you and should be glad to hear occasionally how you are getting on and what you are doing.

Yours sincerely,
Mabel Palmer

24 Clair Avenue, Durban
23 July, 1951

Dear Sister Edista,

I am writing to cancel the enrolment of Lily Moya at Mariannhill with many apologies for all the trouble I have given you. She left Durban last Monday, presumably to join some cousins in Johannesburg, whom she was very anxious to visit. She had an engagement to come and see me that Monday morning, but she never turned up, never went back to Miss Makanya at Umbumbulu where I had arranged for her to spend the holidays, and has never written me any explanation.

I am not on the whole v. sorry to be rid of the responsibility for Lily. She caused trouble wherever she went and her school report is poor. I don't think she could have passed Matric this year and it would have been years before she would have been capable of taking a good teaching post. But I am sorry she has shown herself so incapable of understanding the second chance you so kindly offered her. I have to thank you v. sincerely for all the trouble you took and

I am,
Yours sincerely,
Mabel Palmer

Edith Street,[1]
Sophiatown, Johannesburg
24.7.51

Dear Dr Palmer,

I just write to inform you that I'm very ill. I arrived here on the 17th inst. and that I left Durban and Umbumbulu on the 16th inst.

No news at present,

Greetings to you,
L.P. Moya

Edith Street,
Sophiatown, Johannesburg
24—7—51

Dear Miss Makhanya,

Whatever the case may be I think I should write you this letter.

Many thanks for the time I spent with you, though not very well.[2] I managed to reach this place safely.

No news at present,
Greetings to you all,

I am,
Yours sincerely,
Lily Moya

Edith Street,
Sophiatown, Johannesburg.
26—7—51.

Dear Dr Palmer,

Your letter has been handed to me.

For congenial reasons I had to leave Adams, due to the fact

---

1. For Edith Street, Sophiatown, see Introduction; I have omitted the number for reasons of confidentiality.

2. Probably 'though I am not very well'. For the nature of Lily's illness, see Epilogue, below, pp.143ff.

that I was never meant to be a stone but a human being with feelings, not either an experimental doll.[1]

The books I shall try sending them at the earliest possible.

Before saying anything concerning what you said about the blanket and sheet, I would like to ask you this question. Can you be frank with this Miss Mkhanya's borrowing bussiness of the blanket and sheet? When and how? This new information is beyond my scope of knowledge and your promise.[2]

About Adams, I think in December 1950, if your memory is still good, I told you that I didn't want staying. I had to work and I had clerical vacation[3] to fill. You refused. I really ignored going back and I stayed there in Adams at Mary Lyon House not according to my will. I didn't want staying there. You arranged that at my back. You badly handled me back.[4]

I have no news. I'm very ill.

Hearty greetings.

I am,

P. Lily

P.S. I never wanted a teachers course though you suggested so and insisted that I should stay there.[5]

1. The echo of Shaw's *Pygmalion* was no doubt accidental, but uncanny in this context.
2. It is difficult to know exactly what this episode was about, though from Sibusisiwe's subsequent embarassment it would seem as if Lily was wrongly accused of being responsible for a missing sheet and blanket. See MP to LM, 25.7.51, MP to SM, 8.8.51, and SM to MP, 14.8.51.
3. i.e. vacancy.
4. This would seem to mean either that Mabel had handled her badly, behind her back, or, perhaps, that she had badly — i.e. wrongly — forced her (handed her) back to the school.
5. Given Lily's own request for advice on a subsequent career, the accusation was neither strictly accurate nor fair, but did express her feelings of being manipulated. Mabel was certainly given to making plans for Lily without any consultation.

Dear Miss Kamper,

I am sending you under another cover the blazer that was provided for Lily Moya. I have never paid for it. Why she took it away from Adams, I cannot think nor why she should post it to me in a very badly packed parcel.[1] I hope you will be able to get another student to take it, but if you have to make any reduction in the price because it has been worn, please let me know and I will refund the difference.

I am sorry to hear she was so rude and disobedient to you before she left. I meant to make her write you an apology. But now she has departed without any good-bye either to Miss Makanya or myself to Johannesburg. – and without taking the trouble to know what arrangements were being made for her to go to Mariannhill. So I have cancelled the enrolment at Mariannhill and written to Lily (luckily I had her aunt's address) telling her I will not undertake any further responsibility for her.

She has had the grace to write me a four-line letter, which crossed mine, saying she arrived in Jo'burg on the 17th and is 'very ill'.

I am afraid I was much mistaken in her and am sorry you had so much trouble with her at Adams.

With apologies and kind regards,

Yours v. sincerely,
Mabel Palmer

My dear Dr Palmer,

Saturday a parcel arrived and upon opening it I found two pairs of nice bed socks which you sent me. Many thanks! It was very kind of you to think of me in this way and I appreciate the gift and the spirit lying behind it.

---

1. See LM to MP, 28.6.51 for Lily's explanation. Clearly relationships at Adams had deteriorated to such an extent that Lily could not bring herself to give back the blazer and maintain an air of civility.

I had a letter from Lily. I hope she will come to herself and apologise to you for not coming over to see you when she was in Durban on her way to Jo'Burg.

I am wondering if she is going to return – to go back to school. I rather doubt it though. Well, Dr Palmer, you did all you could for that girl but it seems it is difficult to find out what she really wants.

Thank you again for the gift you sent me.

With kindest regards,
Appreciatively yours,
Sibusisiwe Makhanya

Handwritten note   *8th August*
Wrote also to Miss Scott at Inanda, thanking her and explaining situation

Mabel Palmer

Adams College
8.8.1951

Dear Dr. Palmer,

Thank you for your letter and the parcel containing the blazer. One of our students has taken it and paid £2 for it. As it had been worn a little we made the reduction of 10 sh. I am sorry that all you have done was never appreciated by Lily. She was given a best chance in life and turned it down. I pity her greatly because I feel that she just does not realise, and that is not altogether her fault.

We have started our term well, the students are studying harder this term and that right from the beginning. I am happy in my work, and we pray for God's blessings on it. Thank you for all you have done for us here.

Yours very sincerely,
Elisabeth Kämper

P.S. Tennis Quoit is much loved here.

Dear Miss Makanya,

I do hope you *really* liked the bed-socks. I was getting some for myself and as I wanted to send you a little gift in at least partial recognition of all your kindness to Lily I asked the lady who spoke to me on the phone (Was it Mrs. Reeder?[1]) and she said she thought you would like them. I myself find them wonderfully comforting on these v. cold nights.

Lily has written to me too, the first letter merely giving her address and saying she is 'very ill'. That letter crossed one of mine telling her that I would no longer be responsible for her, nor pay her school-fees. Reasons her very mediocre report (there is no chance, I think, that she will pass matric at the end of this year) and the trouble she has given wherever she went. I am *thankful* to be free from the responsibility for her. Mrs. Reeder (if it was she who spoke to me on the phone) said she helped herself to a blanket and a sheet of yours. I asked her to return them together with the books I lent her.

In her second letter to me, she denies that she took the blanket and sheet and asks who accuses her of it. Would you let me know what is the situation, and whether you have missed anything else? Of course, I will make all that good, if you will let me know the value. Her second letter is not at all a nice one — very truculent and accusing in tone and makes me quite sure that I am wise in getting rid of her. It is a sad conclusion to our relationship but it is a conclusion for which I am thankful. With renewed thanks to you for your help with her.

Yours v. sincerely,
Mabel Palmer

1. i.e. Mrs Reader, the wife of the anthropologist, D. H. Reader, then using Umbumbulu as his base for field research. His book, *Zulu Tribe in Transition: the Makhanya of southern Natal* (Manchester, 1966) is dedicated to 'Sibusisiwe Makhanya, Leader of her people'.

Dear Dr Palmer,

Thank you for your letter. I am glad Lily has at last written to you. I was disgusted when Mrs. Reader told me she had told you about the blanket and sheet. She absolutely had no right to mention this to you. It was not her right at all to talk about my family affairs, moreover, you cannot accuse one unless you have absolute proof. Please forget about this blanket and sheet.

I shall not be sorry, Dr. Palmer, if you part with Lily. You gave her a splendid chance and she has abused it. I shall not at all be surprised if the girl is pregnant.[1] All the accusations she has made to the people were intended to cover up her problem. I began to suspect this when she pressed hard to go to Johannesburg and her general behaviour went to point to one suffering from early pregnancy. I may be wrong. But what Lily wrote in a note to one of the teachers goes, perhaps, to substantiate my assumptions.

I am leaving Thursday, 16th Aug. to attend a Y.W.C.A. Conference in Port Elizabeth. Returning on the 28th.

With kind regards and again thank you for the bed socks.

Yours sincerely,
Sibusisiwe Makhanya

Hope you got my other letter thanking you for the socks.

24 Clair Avenue
Durban
22 Aug. 1951

Dear Lily,

I am sorry to hear you have been ill since your arrival in Johannesburg. What is the matter with you? Have you seen a doctor and how long does he think your illness will last? I myself was not too well last week — tooth-ache and then having to [have] four teeth taken out at once. I now have only

---

1. This was probably not true, but see the Introduction, pp.25,30.

two of my own teeth left and till I get a new set of artificial teeth made I can only eat soft foods and am rather disfigured. Fortunately I can talk all right.

It was not Miss Makanya who told me about the sheet and blanket, but another lady who came to the phone to speak for you. When I mentioned the matter to Miss Makanya, she was quite annoyed and said nothing about it ought ever to have been said to me and that she wished the whole matter to be completely dropped.

I am sending you a p. order for 10/– as a farewell present, as I expect until you get some work you may be short of cash. But will you please use part of it to send my books back. I don't at all mind lending my books, but I do like to get the books back and all the three I lent you are favourites of mine.

I hope I shall soon hear that you are better and able to make plans for the future and that you will tell me what those plans are. I shall always be interested in hearing what happens to you.[1]

Yours v. sincerely,
Mabel Palmer

24 Clair Avenue
Durban
12 Sept. 1951

Dear Miss Kamper

I am glad you were able to sell Lily's blazer and enclose a cheque for 10/– to make up the deficit.

I have heard nothing more from her; I sent her 10/– and asked her to return 3 books of mine which I had lent to her and to tell me what was the matter with her and what the doctor said about her being 'very ill', as she twice assured me she was. But I have no response.

Are we to have the pleasure of seeing you at the opening ceremony of the Medical School on Monday? I think it will be a very interesting occasion.

With kindest regards,

Yours v. sincerely,
Mabel Palmer

1. Lily never wrote to Mabel Palmer again. For what 'happened' to Lily, see the Epilogue.

Provincial Administration of the Cape of Good Hope
Livingstone Hospital
Port Elizabeth
27th November 1951

Dr. Mabel Palmer,
Natal University College
Durban

Dear Madam,

In February of this year Lily Moya applied to train at this hospital as a nurse, her address at that time was Adams College, P.O. Adams Mission College, Natal, from which a letter addressed to her has now been returned "Unknown".

As your name was one which she gave on her form, I thought it possible that you may know her present whereabouts. If you do know her present address I wonder if you would be so kind as to forward the enclosed letter to her as I feel this girl deserves a chance to train if she still wishes to do so.

Thanking you,

Yours faithfully,
B. Drysdale
Matron
p.p. Medical Superintendent

University of Natal, Durban
7th December, 1951

The Matron,
Medical Superintendent
Livingstone Hospital
Port Elizabeth

Dear Madam,

In answer to your letter of the 27th November, 1951, I have to say that the last address I have for Lily Moya is Edith Street, Sophiatown, Johannesburg but as she did not answer the last letter I sent her at that address, I am not certain if she is still there.

However, I am sending on your letter registered post, with

192

the request that if it cannot be delivered it should be returned to me. In that case I will notify you and perhaps if you in turn should hear from Lily Moya you would be kind enough to let me know?

Yours faithfully,
(Dr) Mabel Palmer

Livingstone Hospital
Port Elizabeth
13th December 1951

Dr. Mabel Palmer
P.O. Box 1525
Durban

Dear Madam,

I have to acknowledge with thanks your letter of the 7th instant, the contents of which have been noted. If I should hear from Lily Moya I will be very pleased to let you know.

Thanking you,

Yours faithfully,
B. Drysdale
Matron
p.p. Medical Superintendent

Epilogue

What happened to Lily Moya? For five years after I first discovered the file of letters I tried to find out. Convinced of the significance of the correspondence, I was reluctant to publish it without Lily's permission if she were alive, her family's if she were not. In any case any royalties belonged to Lily. Mabel Palmer and Sibusisiwe Makhanya were both dead.[1] This was − and is − Lily's book. The number of African girls reaching matriculation in the mid-century was so small, and Lily's ability so manifest, that I was hopeful initially that if she were alive and well, I would have no difficulty in tracing her through the closely connected networks of the African intelligentsia. Friends, students, journalists were roped into the search. In 1979 I tried advertising in the African newspapers in both Johannesburg and East London and on Radio Transkei and Radio Bantu − to no avail. Enquiries in the Tsolo district and Umtata were no more successful. I began to lose heart. At the end of 1981, a full-scale article by Barry Streek in the *Daily Despatch* published in East London elicited no comment, despite its detailed quotation of the correspondence. Following its publication in the Johannesburg newspaper, *Rand Daily Mail*, early in the following year, I received a rather devastating, if intriguing, response:

Dear Sir,
It is surprising that you should claim 'a special place in history' for a promiscuous drop out. Such persons (of all races) are not infrequently pushed upstairs as it were, by misguided do-gooders, who eventually come to realize that they are simply wasting time and money. An old story not worth the telling. . . . The crowning fatuity of your article comes when you express a desire to talk to [Lily] . . . . By what right? And why assume she wishes to talk to you?

195

In conclusion, forget about it. Sales will be small and you would be well advised to mind your own business.

Lily (Deflowered)

I was almost about to give up the entire project, especially as this note had no address, when yet another letter arrived. This time it contained rather more positive information. An enquiry directed to one of the mission schools Lily had attended in the 1940s fortuitously discovered one of her mother's sisters teaching there. Lily was indeed alive, and residing with her mother and sister in Soweto. She was, however, far from well; according to the aunt, 'she was very unfortunate in that she could not further her studies due to nerves and therefore was in hospital for a lengthy time . . .'[2]

After considerable soul-searching – was I after all another Mabel Palmer, a 'misguided do-gooder'?, was the letter from 'Lily deflowered' in fact from an embittered Lily unwilling to subject herself to a white researcher? – I decided to go ahead. Through Professor Charles van Onselen, the Director, and the young black oral historians at the African Studies Institute at the University of Witwatersrand we found Lily, her mother and her sister. Far from writing the letter I had received, the family had no knowledge of it at all; its authorship remains a mystery. Contrary to the predictions, the warmth of the family's welcome and support for the project was overwhelming. Without their generosity, confidence and insight, this book could have been neither written nor published. The oral interviews in 1982 and 1984 which Manthe Nkotsoe and Denis Mashabela carried out on my behalf together with my own supplementary meetings with the family in July 1983 and July 1985, facilitated by the late 'Moss' Molepo, enabled me to piece together both the background to the correspondence and this epilogue.

Even before meeting with the family, I had become convinced that Lily's grandparents must have been amongst the relatively prosperous Christian peasantry of the late nineteenth century Eastern Cape. After hearing their account of the family history, I went back to the Anglican records housed in the University of Witwatersrand. To my delight, the very first report that I picked up from St Cuthbert's Mission contained the names of

Lily's maternal grandparents, There were, in addition, descriptions of the grandparents on both sides of the family, which enriched and corroborated, but also modified the account I had been given. The find was exciting, for it provided a useful check on the frailties and fallibilities of the human memory. But the discovery of the written record was important in another and even more rewarding sense. So often, as oral historians, we 'take away' people's history. In a small way, through restoring the descriptions of their kin to the family, I hope to have repaid some of my debt.

For all the joy of discovery, it has proven painful to come to terms with Lily's subsequent story, however, and difficult to write this epilogue. As we have already seen, in the middle of July 1951, Lily ran away from Sibusisiwe Makhanya's home at Umbumbulu. Her mother, Harriet, had finally come up with the ticket in response to a desperate appeal — 'If you don't send me money, you will find me dead'. Once again, despite her lack of experience, Lily managed to find her way to Edith Street, Sophiatown, where her mother was living with her sister.

Once a vibrant African freehold township to the west of Johannesburg, Sophiatown no longer exists. It was destroyed in the mid-1950s under the guise of slum-clearance by the Nationalist government, alarmed by the threat it posed both to *apartheid* and more generally to the authority and control of the state. At the time that Lily arrived there, however, it was the 'swarming, cacophonous, strutting, brawling, vibrating' 'little Paris of the Transvaal' celebrated by Johannesburg's articulate black writers and journalists.[3] Many of its inhabitants were living cheek by jowl in densely-packed, corrugated iron shanties, with whole families sharing a single room, and up to forty people to a single tap and an outside lavatory. For those who lived in it, and loved it, Sophiatown was not simply an impoverished and overcrowded slum, however. The destination of large numbers of Africans pushed off the land in the 1930s and 1940s, and, like Lily's mother, in search of work wherever they could find it, Sophiatown was also the home of South Africa's most sophisticated urban black intelligentsia — and its most sophisticated gangsters.[4] Father Trevor Huddleston, himself working at the mission just a couple of blocks away from Edith Street about the time of Lily's arrival, described the impact the township made on him:

> Sometimes looking up at Sophiatown from the Western Native Township, across the main road, I have felt I was looking at an Italian village somewhere in Umbria. For you do 'look up' at Sophiatown, and in the evening light, across the blue-grey haze of smoke from braziers and chimneys, against a saffron sky, you see close-packed, red-roofed little houses. You see on the farthest skyline, the tall, shapely blue-gum trees . . . You see, moving up and down the hilly streets, people in groups: people with colourful clothes: people who, when you come up to them, are children playing, dancing and standing around the braziers. And above it all you see the Church of Christ the King, its tower visible north, south, east and west, riding like a great ship at anchor upon the grey and gold waves of the town beneath. . . . Sophiatown is not a location . . . It is so utterly free of monotony, in its siting, in its buildings, and in its people. . . . A £3,000 building jostles a row of single-rooms: an 'American' barber shop stands next door to an African herbalist's store, with its dried roots and dust-laden animal hides hanging in the window. You can go into the store to buy a packet of cigarettes and can be served by a Chinaman, an Indian or a Pakistani. You can have your choice of doctors and clinics even.[5]

The excitement and glamour of Sophiatown, as well as the desperate struggles its inhabitants were fighting for survival, were probably lost on Lily, though the Anglican church was to be of enduring importance to her. It was 'the choice of doctors and clinics', however, that was at the centre of her experience of the township. For by the time Lily arrived in Johannesburg she was clearly in a disturbed state. By the end of the month she had written in her last letter to Mabel, 'I am very ill'. And although she did not specify the precise nature of her illness, it was clearly psychiatric. She was withdrawn and depressed, and talked to herself incessantly. The only phrase her sister recalls as intelligible at this time was 'Dr Palmer'. The aunt with whom the family was living found Lily's behaviour so difficult that she felt compelled to turn them out of the house.

For Harriet, unable to pursue her calling as a schoolteacher and forced to undertake domestic work to support her children, Lily's presence created manifest problems. Harriet's employer, a sympathetic Jewish doctor, helped the family rent alternative accommodation and provided free treatment and tablets, but Lily's condition seems to have worsened. One evening, at the end of the year, she rose suddenly, broke through the windows of her mother's newly rented house and ran away to relations living in Orlando West.

White man's tablets had failed. Her relatives now took Lily to a traditional healer, whom the family describe as a 'witch-doctor'.[6] The treatment did not last long. Lily accused the healer of attempting to seduce her, and Harriet swiftly removed her daughter from his clutches. It is impossible to say at this distance whether Lily's allegations were justified, though it was a frequent accusation made against 'traditional' healers practising in Johannesburg at this time, many of them 'quacks', without skill who were simply preying on the weak and gullible.[7] How far Lily's fear of the 'witchdoctors' arose also from her own intense religious feeling and her Anglican background is not clear. In the first decades of this century, there is little doubt that the Anglican Church frowned on traditional healing practices. Thus in 1915, Bishop Callaway wrote to a friend:

> I heard that a catechumen − a married woman − had been very ill, but was getting better ... when she was at her worst, her heathen relatives had gone to the witchdoctor to 'vumusa' − to try to find out what was the cause of sickness etc. Directly the sick woman recovered her understanding, she refused to have anything to do with this, or to accept any of the remedies. It requires a good deal of courage to make a stand of that sort. I came back feeling very happy and encouraged.[8]

Whatever the official church attitude to traditional healing, and the apparent conflict between the church teachings and

African cosmology, it is clear that many Christian Africans integrate indigenous notions of misfortune and sorcery with New Testament ideas of Satan and evil spirits. Moreover, given the inadequate provision and frequent ineffectiveness of western therapy for a variety of afflictions, particularly mental illness and social dis-ease, Africans in South Africa, as elsewhere in Africa, have been and are suitably eclectic and instrumental in their search for health and healing.[9] It is evident that the catechumen Callaway rejoiced over was highly exceptional. For all his Anglican upbringing, Lily's paternal grandfather was renowned as a healer in his own right, as was one of his brothers — and Lily's sister, a highly qualified nurse saw no contradiction in relating the miraculous cures they effected. Despite the possible condemnation of the church, Lily's family sought help wherever they thought they could find it.

Initially, some members of the family, and indeed Lily herself, may have interpreted her illness as *inkathazo* or *ukuthwasa*, the condition afflicting people, usually women, called on by the spirits of the ancestors to become diviners. Many of her symptoms recalled those of the initiate diviners: its onset at adolescense, her abstinence and indeed abhorrence of sexual activity, her disturbed behaviour, her social isolation.[10] Alone and vulnerable, she had desperately sought a 'white mother', only to find herself rejected. Now she had fallen prey to what was commonly called the 'white' illness, white being the colour of the diviner's ritual, regalia and make-up.[11] Nor would the family have regarded their attempt to apprentice Lily to a diviner in order to effect treatment as incompatible with their Christianity, although it would seem that Lily herself rejected the treatment proferred by the doctor she was sent to.[12]

With the failure of the first healer, her uncle next suggested a 'famous *inyanga*'[13] living in Moroka township. This *inyanga* diagnosed Lily's affliction as *amafufunyane*, a form of spirit possession associated with sorcery suffered by women which was first noticed in Natal in the late 1920s and 1930s and somewhat later in the Transkei. Unlike older forms of spirit possession, like *ukuthwasa*, which are often the first sign of clairvoyant power and a 'white' benign affliction, *amafufunyane* and other newer forms of spirit possession, 'black' and dangerous afflictions, appear to be associated at least in their cultural expression with particular recent social stresses.[14]

In the light of Lily's known symptoms, and the stresses she had undergone, the description offered by the anthropologist, Harriet Ngubane, of *amafufunyane* is worth quoting at some length:

> A person with *amafufunyane* in its worst form usually appears mentally deranged. She becomes hysterical, weeps uncontrollably, throws herself on the ground, tears off her clothes, runs around in a frenzy and usually attempts to commit suicide. She reacts violently and aggressively to those who try to calm her. The patient is said to be possessed by a horde of spirits from different racial groups. Usually there may be thousands of Indians or whites, some hundreds of Sotho or Zulu spirits . . . [15]

Unlike possession by ancestral spirits, this form of possession, according to Ngubane, can be linked with psychogenic disorder. She suggests 'that the notion of evil spirit possession is used among the Zulu as an idiom to handle the escalating proportions of psycho-neurosis often associated with failure to cope with the changing way of life in the colonial and post-colonial industrial society.'[16]

The new *inyanga* and his apprentices tried to exorcize the evil spirits he thought Lily had picked up in Natal through substituting special medicines for food, and forcing her to inhale smoke. Appalled by her treatment, Lily ran away yet again: this time to the local clinic, where the healers were reported to the police.

This was to be Lily's last flight. She was now admitted to Sterkfontein, one of the very few mental hospitals available for Africans at that time. Here she was apparently diagnosed as 'schizophrenic'. Certainly, the behaviour her mother and sister reported is consonant with that most frequently described for schizophrenic patients: unintelligible babbling, restlessness, hearing voices, bad-temper.[17] Yet one should also remember that schizophrenia is one of the most frequent and inexact diagnoses of African mental illness in South Africa, but one which the *inyanga* would probably have distinguished from spirit possession. Indeed, even in Britain and the United States, the diagnosis is not always clear and there are those who would maintain that current medical treatments are both inadequate and damaging.[18] Many have argued that labelling the disturbed schizophrenic and prescribing drugs or electroconvulsive therapy may be a way western society absolves itself from trying to understand the bewildering behaviour of

> frightened people trying to make sense of a terrifying and confusing world, ... tormented people trying to cure themselves by immersing themselves in their fantasies, ... angry people protesting against their pain.[19]

Ironically, Lily's access to 'western' mental health care was a sign of her relative privilege. From Sterkfontein, a state-run mental institution, she was moved in 1974 to Randfontein, an old mining compound converted by the Smith Mitchell Company firstly into a TB sanatorium and then into a hospital for chronically ill psychiatric patients, subsidized by the state and run for profit. In all, Lily spent twenty-five years inside these institutions. A shadow of her former self, she emerged in 1976, through the efforts of her sister, a trained nurse, who was dismayed at the conditions she found Lily living under and now felt herself able to take care of her at home. When I met her, she was about fifty years old, and on a hefty regimen of drugs. She barely spoke English and contributed little to any of the interviews, although on very precise matters of fact her memory was quite remarkable.

Lily's tragedy raises in acute form one of the central questions for the social scientist: how to relate individual psychology and psychopathology to social structure and the realities of a specific social order. The nature of her 'breakdown' in particular poses many problems for the historian, problems which are untackled, let alone resolved, in the conventional psychiatric literature, on the one hand, or in most historical literature on the other. In western medicine in general and psychiatry in particular, despite a certain lip-service to the significance of 'social factors', there is a certain reluctance to accept the social aetiology of disease, or the specific cultural forms it may present in. This is in profound contrast to African cosmologies of healing which see most afflictions as intrinsically social and cultural.

As John Janzen shows in relation to the Lower Zaire — and his remarks are widely applicable in southern and central Africa:

> A feature of therapy management in Kongo society is the collective orientation of medicine. The whole diagnostic apparatus is sensitive to the social causes of physiological affliction. African traditional medicine has been criticized by Western missionaries and colonials as superstition that victimizes individuals ostensibly to benefit the social group. But it could be equally well argued that Western medicine focuses on the individual patient and leaves the social context of his illness in pathological chaos. Kongo therapeutic attitudes, like those in many other African societies, are composed to discern the social and psychosomatic causes of illness.[20]

Contemporary western psychiatry tends to stress the biological and genetic aetiology of disease, rather than the social: it is so much easier to measure and to treat illness on an individual basis and so much less threatening to the status quo.[21] Feminist literature, more alert to the socially-constructed, ethnocentric and gender-biased categories of most psychiatric theories, is more helpful, although it is more usually concerned with the plight of First World women. Western feminists have shown the male bias of the profession, and the way in which many psychoanalytical theories are shaped around a male definition of appropriate female behaviour. In South Africa, even in the mental hospital Lily would have seen a white male psychiatrist at very infrequent intervals, although in the final analysis it would have been his views that prevailed.[22] Yet the issue of male definitions of mental illness does not fully address the question which Lily's subsequent life-story raises, and in some sense also answers: what Murray Last has termed the first and most important question to be asked by medical anthropology, 'Who gets sick?'.[23] Confronted with the evidence of these letters and their social context, the historian, at least, can only make sense of the personal and the idiosyncratic through an analysis of social process and social structure.

At one level, Lily's background in the Eastern Cape, and the way she imbibed the lessons of the mission education to which she was exposed lends credence to Fanonesque notions of alienation and psychological colonisation.[24] In a very general sense, her letters indicate an identification with white values and culture which could only lead to a personal crisis of identity when she found herself — almost inevitably — rebuffed. Yet concepts of deracination and psychological alienation are in general too simple to cope with the complexities of colonial psychology and psychopathology. As Margaret Field has shown, for example, frequently so-called culture conflict is in the mind of the western beholder rather than in that of the African.[25] The same Christian heritage can under only slightly different circumstances constitute a source of inner strength and fortitude rather than vulnerability. We have to be open, too, to the possibility that Lily was deliberately overplaying her identification with the values of school and mission in the hopes of enlisting Mabel's support and sympathy. It would be foolish to read all her protestations at face value, despite the undeniable authenticity of her alienation.

Moreover, if there can be little doubt that Lily's alienation and lack of support were socially structured, both as a result of her socialisation through mission education and through the breakup of her family, her breakdown goes beyond generalities about the impact of colonialism and psychological colonisation. Not only do these fail to look at the effects of class, gender or age differentiation on the incidence of disease; they also ignore the variety of individual experience or the different ways individuals reflect on and refract the same experience. Despite the undoubtedly pathogenic nature of her environment, a frightening amalgam of the cruelties structured by colonialism and individual circumstance, to environment must be added the unknown quantity of her personal frailty.

It is impossible to write with certainty of her early childhood experiences. Apart from a few illuminating but elusive comments, Lily was largely silent in the interviews with her family. The drugs on top of twenty-five years in a mental hospital had destroyed much of the liveliness and intelligence so evident in the early letters. Yet her childhood years are suggestive: the death of

204

her father when she was only five or six, her mother's remorseless struggle for a livelihood, and her own frequent moves from school to school were surely traumatic. As we have seen, Harriet was forced to leave the Transkei to seek work in Johannesburg just as Lily entered her final years at school at St John's in Umtata. There she was the only girl in a class of young men, six years younger than the next youngest pupil.[26] Lily's description of herself as 'a helpless orphan' in her letters to Mabel was an apt account of her sense of desolation and loneliness. That she should have been found 'difficult' by her teachers at St John's is, under the circumstances, hardly surprising. The term was to dog her in her stormy career at Adams. It is useful to recall how frequently this word has been applied to intelligent and ambitious women who have refused to accept society's definition of their station in life. Indeed both Mabel and Sibusisiwe were known in their day as 'difficult women'.[27] There can, of course, be little doubt that Lily was 'difficult'. Facing the insecurities and anxieties of puberty on her own, unsupported by either peers or kin, the dice were stacked against her. The extent to which her subsequent problems revolved around her inability to cope at this time with her own adolescent sexuality is perhaps intimated by a clue she herself provided in the course of our interviews in Soweto in 1983.

Thus, in the course of my first discussion with her sister about her visit to the traditional healers, Lily interjected, apparently at random, 'Witchdoctor is menstruation'. On my second visit, when I enquired how she was, she replied, 'I am suffering from menstruation', an unlikely remark contradicted by her sister. The repetition was at least symbolically appropriate, perhaps pinpointing the moment of Lily's greatest distress. For a mother-bereft adolescent trying to come to terms with her own sexuality in a class full of young men, menstruation, the most manifest symptom of puberty and incipient adulthood, may well have constituted a major crisis. In 'traditional' society, menstruation was a time of danger and taboo, during which women were not supposed to even speak to men. It is perhaps not wholly fanciful to suggest that Lily's stress on the syllable 'men' in 'menstruation' was not entirely random. We have already noted how problematic her relationship was with members of the opposite sex: in the letter about 'native girls in the reserves' and the pressures upon them from the returned migrants and from their family to marry; in her escape from her guardian and abhorrence of marriage; in her denunciation of the 'raw schoolboys' and coeducation at Adams; in her flight from the advances of the witchdoctor — whether real or imagined.

The contradictions between Lily's notions of the 'good woman' imbibed from the Anglican mission and the African emphasis on marriage and motherhood were acute. Recently the feminist scholar, Jill Mathews, has suggested that the existence of a 'maelstrom of changing and contradicting ideals' of femininity mean that a woman's

> pursuit of any, let alone a unified, ideal of femininity
> . . . must inevitably lead to failure at some point or another.
> She will inevitably transgress some norms of femininity no matter how diligently she tries to conform to a true pattern.
> Indeed, such transgression is structured into the very pursuit itself, since the individual desires an internally consistent femininity, whereas the ideal is socially structured as inconsistent.[28]

For Lily, these contradictions were to explode when confronted further by the conflicting ideals of femininity held by Mabel Palmer and Sibusisiwe Makhanya.

This is not to say her breakdown was simply an adolescent crisis over sexuality. There were additional sources of strain. With her close family gone and with few friends, Lily staked her all on her scholastic achievements. Intensely ambitious, and finding self-identification through her intellectual ability, one can only imagine that her failure in the matriculation examinations in 1948 and again in 1949 must have come as a severe blow. Desperately she tried to find in Mabel the mother-figure she lacked. And Mabel's generosity partly drew her on. Yet Mabel was fitted by neither temperament nor experience to fulfil a maternal, or indeed even a supportive, role. Perhaps sensing the dangers of Lily's dependence, she reacted with her typical acerbity, and explicitly dissociated herself emotionally from her charge. There is no indication in her letters to Lily that she had even an inkling of the suffering experienced by her 'poor little protegée'. As her last lifeline was cut through Mabel's rejection, Lily became depressed, and finally suffered a psychotic breakdown, her last way perhaps of seeking 'the support, sympathy and attention that depressed people often long for'.[29]

Whatever the relationship between individual psychology and social structure and whatever the precise diagnosis of Lily's disturbed behaviour, whether it was the intense depression manifested in spirit possession diagnosed by the traditional healer, or the schizophrenic illness she was treated for by the mental hospitals — and the two are by no means mutually exclusive — there can be little doubt that her incarceration for twenty-five years in a mental institution gravely worsened her condition. Quite apart from the specific repressions of mental institutions for blacks in South Africa, the evidence is overwhelming that prolonged confinement in the 'total' institution of the asylum tends to exacerbate rather than heal mental illness. Social deprivation, uncertainty and coercion are the hallmarks of mental hospitals in many parts of the world; in the absence of a supportive therapeutic community, confinement alone was only likely to increase the anxiety and withdrawal of the unhappy Lily.[30]

In the 1950s the psychiatric services available to Africans in South Africa were — as they still are — both primitive and few and far between. At the time of Lily's admission to Sterkfontein, mental health was still a very low public health priority and even white psychiatric patients suffered from neglect. Over the next twenty-five years, services for mentally-ill whites improved greatly, with the establishment of new Departments of Psychiatry in the teaching hospitals in the 1950s and the expansion of beds and outpatient facilities.[31] For blacks there was virtually no expansion in the state provision of mental health facilities — justified on the grounds of lack of demand.[32] As late as 1979, three years after Lily had been released from their care, there were only 5 000 state-provided beds for mentally disturbed Africans in South Africa. By that time, the state had handed over the care of a large number of chronically ill patients to a private company, Smith Mitchell & Company, and it was to their facility at Randfontein that Lily, by then labelled 'chronically ill' had been transferred in 1974.

Detailed notes by members of the Committee of the American Psychiatric Association who visited South Africa in 1979 at the invitation of Smith Mitchell and the Department of Health suggest that she may well have found this an improvement on her position in Sterkfontein. Nevertheless, as the Committee points out in its report:

> Since Smith Mitchell's *raison d'être* is to provide care for less than it would cost the Government, it adheres to the apartheid labour practices used by the Government. . . . since Smith Mitchell's goal is to maximize profits, it is clear that, without close supervision, it might have a strong incentive to cut costs even to the detriment of patients.[33]

Through the 1970s and since, psychiatric care for Africans in South Africa has been a matter of widespread international concern: the American Psychiatric Association delegation found, for example,

> medical practices which were unacceptable and which resulted in the needless deaths of Black South Africans. We found that the medical and psychiatric care provided for Blacks was grossly inferior to that provided for Whites.[34]

Four years later, a WHO report on *Health and Apartheid*, recorded that 'over-crowding, a depersonalizing custodial regime, and deprivation of elementary amenities and possessions' characterize black psychiatric institutions.[35] Therapy consisted mainly of neuroleptic drugs and simple occupational therapy, some of it thinly disguised free labour. Diagnosis was primitive — not surprisingly considering the paucity of trained psychiatric staff and their lack of linguistic skills. As late as 1982, there was only one black psychiatrist practising in South Africa. As Lily's experience demonstrates, discharge rates were extremely low, although again significantly her release in 1976 mirrors a shift in policy and a considerable increase in the discharge figures from Randfontein in that year and subsequently.

Thus to the frequent depersonalization and humiliation

experienced by the mentally ill in the 'total institution' of the mental hospital were added the discrimination experienced by Africans in South Africa's psychiatric institutions.

Yet for Lily, being an 'inmate' was perhaps no new experience. Today she makes an explicit link between the boarding schools and the mental hospitals she has experienced. Commenting on her inability to form enduring friendships, she explained, 'My life was a transfer. I was transferred from St Cuthbert's to Shawbury, from Shawbury to St Matthew's, from St Matthew's to St John's, from St John's to Adams, and from Adams to Sterkfontein, from Sterkfontein to Randfontein and from Randfontein to Soweto'. It had all become a seamless web. In another interview, she maintained, 'Mrs Palmer gave me scholarship to Sterkfontein'.[36] The perceptions are symbolically piquant.

NOTES

1 In 1958 and 1971 respectively.
2 Pers. comm. 26 May 1982. To preserve confidentiality it is not possible to cite the name.
3 Can Themba, 'Requiem for Sophiatown', in *The Will To Die* (London, 1972), 104, 107. Cf. also Lewis Nkosi, *Home and Exile* (London, 1965); M. Tlali, *Miriam at Metropolitan* (Johannesburg, 1975); E. Patel, *The World of Nat Nakasa* (Johannesburg, 1975).
4 This description of Sophiatown draws heavily on T. Lodge, *Black Politics in South Africa since 1945* (London and New York, 1984), chapter 4, which also deals with the reasons for its destruction and the African resistance to it. For the origins of Sophiatown and its early history, see A. Proctor, 'Class struggle, segregation and the city: a history of Sophiatown, 1905–1940' in B. Bozzoli, *Labour, Townships and Protest* (Johannesburg, 1979).
5 Trevor Huddleston, *Naught for Your Comfort* (Johannesburg and London, 1956), 121–2, 126–7. Part of this is also cited in Lodge, op.cit., 94.
6 There are two kinds of traditional healer in African society in South Africa: a diviner or diagnostician, the *isangoma* or *isanusi*, and a herbalist or *inyanga*. It is not clear to which category – if either – this 'witchdoctor' belonged, but if the family members thought Lily was an initiate diviner (see below), he would have been an *isanusi*.

7   Many so-called traditional healers especially in the towns had little
    of the traditional training in herbal and social medicine of their
    precolonial counterparts. Some nonetheless made – and make –
    very considerable fortunes. They are called on to 'heal' a wide
    variety of afflictions. Thus, as S. Feierman points out in his compre-
    hensive bibliography on *Health and Society in Africa* (Waltham,
    1978), African healers often treat not only physical illness, but also
    'lovers' jealousy, business failure and potential defeat in football'. In
    addition to the conventional literature on specific and defined
    diseases, the bibliography lists studies of witchcraft and sorcery,
    Islamic and Christian healing cults, spirit possession and ethno-
    medicine.

8   *Occasional News*, October, 1915. Extracts from Fr Callaway's letters,
    Whitsun, 1915.

9   For the distinctions Africans draw between western and indigenous
    healing practices, see H. Ngubane, *Body and Mind in Zulu Medicine*
    (New York, 1977); for the eclecticism elsewhere in Africa, see
    J. Janzen, *The Quest for Therapy in Lower Zaire* (Berkeley, 1978).
    For African cults of affliction and 'the complex and shifting notions
    of healing' in African society see T. Ranger, 'Healing and society
    in colonial southern Africa', paper presented to the Society for
    Social History and Medicine, 1978.

10 I am grateful to Professor John Blacking of Belfast who pointed this
    possibility out to me most cogently at a seminar in Belfast in May,
    1985, Dr Richard Werbner of Manchester also very perceptively
    described Lily 'as someone symbolically distancing herself from
    herself, someone who would be a changeling in myth, a subject for
    spirit possession in ritual, or for alienation and "adoption" in the
    absence of myth and ritual'. Pers. comm. (31 Jan. 1983). For a
    description of the symptoms of *ukuthwasa*, see B.A. Pauw, *Chris-
    tianity and Xhosa Tradition* (Cape Town, London and New York,
    1975), 166. Also John Blacking, pers. comm.

11 Pauw, *Christianity and Xhosa Tradition*, 166.

12 For the integration of the two belief systems and the continued
    consultation of traditional healers by educated Christian Xhosa,
    see 165–9, 251–60.

13 See Note 6 above.

14 Ngubane, *Body and Mind*, 142–6; the substance of this chapter is
    also reproduced in H. Sibisi (Ngubane), 'Spirit possession in Zulu
    cosmology', in M.G. Whisson and M. West (eds.), *Religion and
    Social Change in Southern Africa* (Cape Town and London, 1975),
    54–5. Pauw, Ibid. 251.

15 Ngubane, *Body and Mind*, 144.

16 Ibid. 149.

17 Phyllis Chesler, *Women and Madness*, (New York, 1972), 51–2.

18 The diagnosis differs even between the United States of America and Europe. The classic study by David Rosenhan in the United States, in which eight psychologists with no history of mental illness had themselves admitted to a mental institution on complaining of hearing faint voices, and were then diagnosed as schizophrenic despite normal behaviour thereafter perhaps illuminates some of the problems of the diagnosis. Cited in D. Taylor, 'Madness and badness', *New Internationalist*, issue no. 132, February, 1982, p8.

19 Ibid. 9.

20 *The Quest for Therapy in Lower Zaire*, 9.

21 Much of the contemporary 'cultural critique' of medicine as it has developed in the western world focuses on its insufficiency in precisely this area. See, for example, John and Barbara Ehrenreich (eds.) *The Cultural Crisis of Medicine* (New York, 1978).

22 In the late 1970s, in state-run black psychiatric hospitals, each full-time psychiatrist was responsible for over 600 patients. At Randfontein (Lily's second psychiatric hospital) there were two part-time psychiatrists to 3200 patients. At that time, there was no African psychiatrist in the whole of South Africa. *Apartheid and Health*, 240, 247.

23 'The presentation of sickness in a community of non-Muslim Hausa', in J.B. Loudon (ed.), *Social Anthropology and Medicine* (London, 1976). A.S.A. Monograph, no.13.

24 For a superb exposition of Fanon's psychiatric and political writings, see J. McCulloch, *Black Soul White Artifact: Fanon's clinical psychology and social theory* (Cambridge University Press, 1983). I am grateful to Richard Rathbone for drawing this and the following reference to my attention.

25 M.J. Field, *Search for Security: an ethno-psychiatric study of rural Ghana* (London, 1960).

26 I am grateful to Rosalie Kingwill of Umtata for finding the matriculation reports for me which show this.

27 As R. Plante's recent account of Germain Greer, Sonja Orwell and Jean Rhys, entitled *Difficult Women* (London, 1983) suggests, it is a term which has been affixed to many creative and intelligent women who assert themselves against their allotted role in life.

28 Jill Julius Matthews, *Good and Mad Women* (North Sydney, Australia and Hemel Hempstead, Herts. 1984), 17–18.

29 Ngubane, *Body and Mind*, 149.

30 Ibid. 149. Cf. also 'Because *ufufunyane* patients are believed to be still susceptible to *ufufunyane* attacks if provoked or annoyed, those around them must take special care to avoid situations that might make *ufufunyane* recur. . . . If we accept that spirit possession

of the *ufufunyane* type is symptomatic of various forms of extreme depression or nervous breakdown, precautions taken become understandable, as people who have had such mental confusion become vulnerable in situations of stress and strain. They must take care and avoid situations of anxiety or strenuous mental exercize.' (149)

31 See M. Minde, 'History of mental health services in South Africa: services since Union', *South African Medical Journal*, 15.3.1975, 405–9 and 'History of mental health services in South Africa: the future of mental health services', *SAMJ*, 16.4.1977, 549–553.

32 See the graph, for example, in R.P. no 29/1964: *Annual Report of the Commissioner for Mental Health year ended 31st December, 1962*, p.3, which shows a doubling of the actual numbers of black patients (4620 Africans, coloureds and Indians) admitted to mental hospitals, but only a marginal increase in the beds per 100 000 of the population (from 22 to about 34 per 100 000), compared with an increase from 58 to 108 per 100 000 for whites.

33 The report of the visit of the American Psychiatric Association to South Africa was issued as an Official Action in the *American Journal of Psychiatry*, July 1980. It is significant that the APA delegation were not allowed to make the same detailed investigation of state mental health facilities as they could of the Smith Mitchell & Company's privately run mental institutions. I am grateful to Professor Alan Stone of Harvard Law School who headed the delegation for access to its notes.

This section is based more generally on this report and the papers of the delegation, as well as WHO, *Health and Apartheid* (Geneva, 1983), 230–248. See also 'The Evaluation of the Smith Mitchell & Co. mental health facilities' by Stanley Platman and Vera E. Thomas, 1981–2 (APA Papers, Harvard Law School). I have refrained from citing the actual information provided by Lily and her sister about conditions at Sterkfontein and Randfontein, because the South African Mental Health Amendment Act of 1976 prohibits the publication of 'false information concerning the detention, treatment, behaviour or experience in an institution of any patient or person who was a patient, or concerning the administration of any institution'. As the APA delegation noted, this inhibits the free discussion of mental institutions and psychiatric practices in South Africa and makes it difficult to get accurate data. There was nothing in what they said which would entail a substantial modification of the WHO or APA findings, although they and I would stress the dedication of individual doctors and nurses.

34 Report of the American Psychiatric Association visit to South Africa, 1979.

35 WHO, *Health and Apartheid*, 243.

36 The anthropologist, John Blacking, suggested in conversation (May 1985) that Lily may in fact have seen Sterkfontein as part of her 'medical training' to be a diviner, in the same way as the schools were a means to the same end. In view of her aversion to and flight from the traditional healers, and her continued staunch adherence to the Anglican church, I find this unlikely, although it is an interesting idea.

Index

215

The Women's Press is a feminist publishing house. We aim to publish a wide range of lively, provocative books by women, chiefly in the areas of fiction, literary and art history, physical and mental health and politics.

To receive our complete list of titles, send a large stamped addressed envelope. We can supply books direct to readers. Orders must be pre-paid in £ sterling with 60p added per title for postage and packing (70p overseas). We do, however, prefer you to support our efforts to have our books available in all bookshops.

The Women's Press, 34 Great Sutton Street, London EC1V 0DX

Farida Karodia
Daughters of the Twilight

Meena, youngest daughter of an Indian father and 'Coloured'
mother, grows up in a suffocating backwater in South Africa in
the 1950s. These are the years when apartheid is under
construction and Meena, quiet and introspective, watches her
family respond in different ways as the pressure on their lives
rapidly mounts. Yasmin, her sister, escapes to a private school,
imitating the 'white' social world of riding lessons and 'coming-
out' balls, which leaves her ill-prepared for the realities she
must face; her father refuses to believe that 'the law' will really
dispossess him of his home and business; and her mother
desperately juggles the day-to-day needs of the family with
ever-threatening poverty.

Yet even as the family is robbed of its home and livelihood, and
Yasmin's cruel tragedy begins to cause the family to
disintegrate, the overpowering impression is one of the
strength, dignity and indomitable spirit of women in adversity.

Fiction   £3.95
ISBN: 0 7043 4017 8
Hardcover   £7.95
ISBN: 0 7043 5007 6

Ellen Kuzwayo
Call Me Woman

Ellen Kuzwayo now lives in Soweto, the sprawling black
township outside Johannesburg. But she grew up in the 1920s
and 30s on her family's beautiful farm near Thaba 'Nchu in the
Orange Free State. That land was forcibly 'purchased' by the
South African Government in the 1970s, as part of its policy of
removing so-called 'black spots' from areas allocated to whites.

The author writes about the women in her family, the girls she
taught as a young woman, her colleagues in social and political
life, and the women who shared political imprisonment with
her in the 1970s.

Call Me Woman is destined to prove a classic of rediscovered
women's history.

Autobiography/Politics   £4.95
ISBN: 0 7043 3936 6
Hardcover   £9.95
ISBN: 0 7043 2848 8